Practical Ways to a Powerful Personality

"There's no sense in blaming yourself for the fact that you can't enjoy sex, or that you lack confidence," says Dr. Weinberg. "What you must examine are your actions, ways of living that drain your spirit and confidence." This internationally acclaimed book shows how you can change your attitudes through your actions and overcome fear, anxiety and shame.

Dr. George Weinberg is a psychotherapist in private practice. He has a Master's degree in English and a doctorate in clinical psychology. He is the author of *Society and the Healthy Homosexual*.

"Shows how by judicious choice of correct actions we can rid our personalities of fear, anxiety, shame, correct our attitudes and develop a powerful personality."

Nagpur Times

"Interesting and informative..." **Amrit Bazar Patrika**

"A book that everyone must read." **MP Chronicle**

"Widely acclaimed....a classic book. Highly useful and practical."

Pioneer

Also in
Orient Paperbacks

Treasury of Courage & Confidence/ Norman Vincent Peale
Why Some Positive Thinkers Get Powerful Results/Norman Vincent Peale
The Conquest of Worry/Swett Marden
Effective Public Speaking/N.D.Batra
Success in 30 Days/A.P.Pereira
Achieve Success and Happiness/A.P.Pereira
Tough Times Never Last, But Tough People Do/Robert H. Schuller

Practical Ways to a Powerful Personality

George Weinberg

Orient Paperbacks
DELHI | MUMBAI | HYDERABAD

ISBN 81-222-0091-5

1st Indian Edition 1977
12th Printing 2002

Practical Ways to a Powerful Personality
(Originally published as *Know Yourself Help Yourself*
by *St. Martins Press, USA*)

© St. Martins Press, USA

Cover design by Vision Studio

Published in arrangement with
St. Martins Press, USA

Published by
Orient Paperbacks
(A division of Vision Books Pvt. Ltd.)
Madarsa Road, Kashmere Gate, Delhi-110 006

Printed in India at
Rakesh Press, Delhi-110 028

Cover Printed at
Ravindra Printing Press, Delhi-110 006

Thank you,
Alice Fennessey,
for your many judgments
about the writing of this book.
Thank you,
Tom McCormack and Dr. C. A. Tripp,
for your extensive advice and encouragement.
Finally, thanks to
Dr. Louis Ormont,
as profound in his love of his patients
as in his understanding of them,
whose approach to psychoanalysis
emphasizes actions.

Contents

Chapter One: Our Most Important Cues — 9
Chapter Two: Some Ways to Know Your Feelings — 15
Chapter Three: The Necessary Starting Place for Self-Help — 28
Chapter Four: The Action Approach — 32
Chapter Five: The Interaction and the Vantage-Point Effects — 37
Chapter Six: Direct Effect — 46
Chapter Seven: The Process of Change — 58
Chapter Eight: A Story from the Past — 66
Chapter Nine: Trauma and What We Can Do about It — 75
Chapter Ten: Paranoia — 88
Chapter Eleven: The Fourth Effect—Recognition — 120
Chapter Twelve: Some Comparisons of the Effects — 128
Chapter Thirteen: Fear and Anxiety — 138
Chapter Fourteen: Backward Inference — 150
Chapter Fifteen: Habits and Compulsions — 157
Chapter Sixteen: Love Without Obstacles — 182
Chapter Seventeen: Inconsistency: Real or Imagined? — 193
Chapter Eighteen: Rehearsal — 207
Chapter Nineteen: How to Make a Complaint — 213
Chapter Twenty: Personal Values and Personality — 232
Chapter Twenty-one: Mental Health and Personal Goals — 237
Chapter Twenty-two: Summary and Some Conclusions — 241

CHAPTER 1

Our Most Important Cues

I WAS A nervous child. When adults told me to relax, I would immediately get more nervous and start to tremble. Not until I grew older did I realize that the simple instruction to relax was making me angry. The reason was I didn't know how to follow such an instruction. Or even how to try to follow it.

How do you change an inner state? No one explains to us how to do this the way they instruct us in multiplication, and no one demonstrates the process, so we have no way of copying it. I think a valid starting place is the acknowledgment that people often cannot change their inner states merely by acts of will. If the problem were always that easy, I'd instruct all my patients to do so, and send them home. As it is, however, nearly all my patients and I reach a quick understanding that simple instructions from me would not be enough to help them. Whatever the person's problem, he has almost surely been told before coming to me that he's taking things too seriously or that he would enjoy his life more if he'd only relax. In effect, he's been told to change his adrenalin rate. He's been told to exercise choice over feelings not subject to choice. One might as well tell him not to fear going to war, or not to believe in an afterlife, or to believe in an afterlife. Something more than the person's will is needed for him to produce such changes in attitude.

It was only later on, I think when I took a psychology course in college, that I realized our inability to switch off our feelings at will isn't a curse. Our feelings are cues that someone is treating us well or badly, or that we're treating ourselves well or badly. As with all cues, it serves us to maintain continuous access to them. At social gatherings I have occasionally tried to explain to someone how psychotherapy works, and have once or twice gotten a sinking feeling which told me I ought to drop the subject. My anxiety has told me I wasn't in an easy give-and-take relationship, and that in response to questions I must have been trying to defend my field and justify myself. Usually, I very much enjoy talking about my field, especially to an intelligent listener with an honest interest, or even an honest skepticism. But sometimes I meet a person who is committed to not accepting my answers because he enjoys the role of having me strain to make contact with him while he sits back in judgment.

Of all the cues that might enable me to distinguish between the two sorts of people, my own anxiety is by far the best. When my anxiety tells me to stop explaining myself, and I look back over the conversation, I can nearly always see why I'd begun to press so hard. The person either hasn't responded to what I've said, he's been smug, or he's repeated his questions, not acknowledging that I've answered them, and not having bothered to tell me that he disagreed. I have learned to be thankful for the feeling that warns me to stop.

Therapists are specially trained to identify their attitudes toward their patients, the theory being that when you know what you're feeling you are less likely to act irrationally than when you don't. During an initial interview a girl in her twenties told me that she couldn't form lasting relationships, and that the one friend she had, a girl whom she had known for years, had recently stopped returning her calls. Within a few minutes she offered the information that one of my paintings was crooked, that my toilet didn't work well enough, and that my waiting room was too small. If I hadn't been slightly annoyed by her swarm of suggestions, all of which she considered constructive, perhaps I wouldn't have understood so keenly how her escorts had felt just before deciding not to see her again. My annoyance, which at its height was no more than momentary pique, helped keep vivid my appreciation of one way in which this girl was destroying relationships.

I remember at another time using my feelings to grasp a problem that I might never have properly understood without them. The patient, another girl in her twenties, was due at six o'clock. She was already ten minutes late when I heard footsteps out in the hall, which I took to be hers. However, it turned out that the woman outside was not my patient; I heard her walk past my office and toward the elevator which came and took her upstairs. And then I caught a very unusual reaction which, luckily, I identified. It was relief. I didn't want to think about this reaction; it was unusual for me, since ordinarily I feel very close to my patients, look forward to seeing them, and enjoy working with them. Why had I felt relief when I heard the elevator arrive? Did I dislike the girl who was due? No, I liked her. Yet it was undeniable that I wanted her to be late, or to cancel the hour completely. I asked myself what thoughts about her came into my mind, and the first thought that came to me was I was letting her down.

She had come to see me only about five times and already I was feeling symptoms of the belief that I wasn't helping her fast enough. I asked myself where this belief had come from. Was there something I should have been doing that I neglected to do! Then the explanation for my feeling came to me: The girl had told me that different men, her father, her husband, her boss, had proved disappointments to her. She had done all that had been expected of her and more, and they had failed to fulfill the promises that they made. She had put faith in each of these people, had worked hard and done what they wanted, but in the end each of them disregarded her needs. Her father had disregarded them by not spending time

12

with her when she was young, her husband by not making sex enjoyable for her, her boss by not volunteering a raise though she gave up lunch many times when he needed her help. Clearly I was to be the next disappointment to her, and I was already feeling twinges about being incompetent.

In our first session the girl had told me that she'd hesitated for months before calling me up, adding that now she was glad she had come. She intimated that she would do anything that I wanted her to; she had a habit of leaning forward and listening with obvious attentiveness to whatever I said; she answered all questions carefully and slowly, and often nodded agreement, showing me that she was perfectly cooperative. Though nothing had changed as yet, she assured me that she was certain that I could help her and that she'd made an excellent choice in coming to me. No wonder I'd felt concern over being incompetent to help her! She had established the premise that any failure of therapy would be mine, and I had accepted the premise without examining it.

By studying my reaction to her, I had identified her tactic with me. Now I couldn't wait for my patient to come. I had a much clearer understanding of what her problem was and, though I wanted to collect more data before describing the problem to her, I was not again subtly victimized by her approach, and I didn't become the next disappointment to her.

Your feelings are your cues in the interpersonal world, cues that a relationship is wrong or right, cues that your own behavior is furthering your interests or pushing you away from your aspirations, cues that other people love you and accept your activities and values or that they want to change you, cues that they're rooting for you or that they're exploiting you. If you want to alter a feeling or attitude, like chronic depression or fear, the first step must *not* be to deny its existence but to try to identify the feeling, and to describe to yourself in as much detail as possible the thoughts evoked in you by the feeling. Many people have told me that as they walked down the aisle or signed an important job contract years ago, they somehow knew, or "sensed" as they usually put it, that they were making a tragic and difficult-to-reverse mistake. However, because they didn't trust, or didn't want to trust, their misgivings at the time, they persisted in the activity they had started and only years later were forced to acknowledge that if they'd listened to their own emotions they might well have made a better choice.

CHAPTER 2

Some Ways to Know Your Feelings

Here are some ways to identify what your true feelings are.

1. Try to accept the fact that you'll hold nearly every attitude at some time, even toward the people closest to you.

Most people know that if they're furious at a spouse, this doesn't mean that they hate him or wouldn't rush to his side if he needed them. However, many believe that a sudden welling of rage toward a child who's awakened them just after they've fallen asleep is a symptom of severe difficulty. This is not so. Most if not all mothers have at some time felt the impulse to do violence to their children. Such impulses, in and of themselves, don't disqualify a mother from being capable or kind. You may momentarily feel enraged at anyone who thwarts you, and acknowledging that you feel this way is the best safeguard against acting irrationally. You're alive, and being alive means that you have a spectrum of feelings toward nearly everyone, including the people you love.

Whereas the feeling of rage may not be costly at all, the attempt to deny that the feeling exists may have repercussions very harmful to you. Since every attitude is connected with others you hold, you can't dull yourself to particular attitudes without dulling yourself to other attitudes too. We've all had sexual urges toward people completely out of bounds, and toward people whose very names we didn't know; and we can hardly obscure from ourselves the knowledge we have such feelings without dulling our responsiveness elsewhere. The person who tells me he never felt sexually attracted to someone he saw in a film is reporting in effect that he has lowered the intensity of his sexual feelings, probably including feelings about his legal mate. No feeling in itself is wicked. However, the attempt to deny the existence of any of our feelings may dull their intensity and makes it harder for us to identify what they are.

2. Try to identify physical and verbal signs of how you feel.

Most of us have physical danger signs, leaning forward in our seat, biting a lip, or covert signs like dizziness, which, depending on who we are, tell us the sorts of feelings arising in us. A friend of mine never uses the word "silly" except when he's annoyed and doesn't yet know he's annoyed. He described a law as silly, and a policeman who stopped him when he didn't think he was going at an illegal speed as silly.

Which of your habits can serve as a cue to how you feel? Do you slow down your rate of speech, or become excessively polite, when you feel a murderous rage coming on? Or do you involuntarily say you're not a violent man?

3. Understand that if you have a feeling you don't have to act on it.

Throughout the ages people have argued that feelings overwhelmed them. Crimes of passion have gone unpunished on the theory that our emotions can flood us and overpower our will. If we assume that a feeling can force us to act, we must naturally dread many feelings and not want to know about them. We may come to deny the existence of rage or envy, or even love, where we wish to avoid decisions toward which these feelings impel us. To do so is a mistake. The more we learn about our feelings, the better prepared we are to resist our inclinations to act in ways we decide would be harmful to us.

4. Don't set your sights on becoming a person who's never afraid.

An eight-year-old girl to whom I once gave an I.Q. test defined the word "courage" in a way that was very instructive to me. "Courage" she said, "is the ability to act when you're afraid." By now the girl is twenty-three and, if she has preserved that belief, think what a wonderful gift it would make to the people in her life. Someone might tell her that he was afraid to ask for a raise, or to walk through a dangerous neighborhood, without losing esteem in her eyes. Intimacy is possible only among those who realize that fear is part of life.

Don't let the American hero, as depicted on stage and screen, become an ideal for you. Offstage, the actors who play the parts are as fearful as anyone else, and I include those who star in Western roles.

5. Be especially careful not to misrepresent your attitudes when trying to justify a decision.

It's when trying to justify choices we've made, or plan to make, that we're most tempted to misrepresent our attitudes. Once we've depicted ourselves as weary, disappointed, or desperately in love, we work at believing that our characterizations of ourselves are accurate. To the extent that we succeed, we dull our awareness of what our real feelings are. We pay the price in unexpected places. For instance, the practice of doing business at lunch is a potentially dangerous one. Are you looking forward to lunch, or to being with someone whose values you abhor but whose friendship is useful to you? In attempting to make such lunches companionable, we tend to obscure the distinction and make it hard to separate people we like from people we need.

6. Any act you're ashamed of provides some motivation for you not to know how you feel.

Remember the line of Macbeth: "To know my deed, 'twere best not know myself."

7. Don't mistrust feelings simply because you can't account for them.

Women often tell me they have gone on dates with men, sometimes gone to bed with them, because they couldn't put together an argument for not seeing these men anymore. It's a standard trick of boors to demand that other people explain their positions, not out of interest in what the explanation will be, but because they know that some people forgo their preferences when they can't account for them.

"Why won't you see me again?" "Why are you changing your mind?" "Why won't you kiss me good night?"

Not knowing the answer *doesn't* imply that the decision you contemplate is unjustified. Where we can identify our misgivings about some decision, so much the better for us. But our inability to explain a preference does not mean that it has no satisfactory explanation. Feelings existed long before the formal study of psychology was born, and feelings don't depend for their existence on our being able to account for them.

8. Discuss your feelings only with people you trust.

Your feelings are precious. There is danger in discussing them with people who may judge you adversely by what you report. You may very likely sense this danger when describing your feelings, in which case your impulse will be to misrepresent them, paving the way for you to misrepresent them to yourself.

9. Don't pretend to be broad-minded as a way of avoiding the discomfort of being angry.

"To understand all is to forgive all." That was Victor Hugo's point of view. However, the human body often refuses to substitute understanding for pain and rage. Are you really forgiving someone for an act because you understand his motive, or are you readily assuming that his act was warranted because you don't want to acknowledge being angry with him? If the latter is the case, your rage will turn to depression, your depression to apathy, and the apathy will surely spread. Anger as a reaction to being wronged is not neurotic. The substitution of pseudo-insight for anger is a sanction of your oppressor and a strong vote against yourself.

Some people find it easier to become angry when a friend is wronged than when they themselves are wronged. They are better friends of other people than of themselves. From what I can tell, the philosophy that it's best to bury anger immediately—even at outrages—is propounded mainly by people lacking in confidence or energy. The person who, out of principle, won't become angry is probably incapable of allegiance to himself or anyone else.

By the way, beware of people who tell you strings of anecdotes about how other people abuse them, and who never seem rattled while telling these stories. As soon as you become angry and protest on their behalf, they become calmer than ever and look at you as though you were having a seizure. Because they're afraid of their own reaction, they tell you their "victim stories" to borrow your anger, and then while you rant for their sake, they feel superior to you.

10. Drugs and tranquilizers.

Man has long enjoyed altering his outlook by the use of drugs. Primitive tribes credited mescaline with bringing them closer to God, and many people describe various drugs as giving them religious experiences. The idea that drugs give people profoundly important insights into themselves is also made. People who make discoveries about themselves under drugs can seldom report them in such a way as to convince others that they are truly discoveries. Yet the claim may well be valid. The very argument made is that the drug experience is deeply personal and essentially unreportable.

There can be no doubt that certain drug experiences afford new vantage points. But I would guess the main reason for people's taking nearly any drug is the emotional state being sought. There should be no embarrassment about saying that this pleasurable state is what is wanted, no need to glorify it or rationalize it by calling the state metaphysical or educational. If very hard work was needed to reach the new perspectives produced by drugs, I doubt that most users would pursue these insights by diligent effort. In other words, the very wish to achieve new perspectives is reinforced by the ease of seeking them by drugs. The determination of whether drugs provide new and important insights is complicated by another frequent effect. A sense of elation makes trivial ideas seem like profound new discoveries. It is hard to distinguish real insights from such illusions.

The injuriousness of getting hooked on an addictive drug is beyond question. The person almost always gives his access to the drug, such as heroin or morphine, the highest priority in his life.

As for tranquilizers, the millions of people who down a handfull of pills as soon as they feel upset are paying for their remedy. True, their relief is quick. But it is temporary. The cost is that they lose contact with the sense of distress which they felt, and which, if properly interpreted, could have been a great help to them.

The danger of tranquilizers is that they dull discontent. Discontent is the gasoline that goads us to ask for what we want in life. And so the price of taking tranquilizers regularly is that you are apt to settle for something short of what you might be able to achieve.

11. Beware the extensive use of distractants.

New York City is filled with people who walk through the streets holding transistor radios close to their heads. One gets the impression that if the station piping the music to them were bombed, these people would die immediately. Strictly speaking, they aren't *dulling* their underlying attitudes; they're distracting themselves so that they won't have to think about their lives. One of the best procedures for learning what our underlying attitudes are is to sit alone in a room and to think about them, and one of the surest ways to prevent ourselves from identifying them is to arrange for continuous distractions. Whereas drugs correspond to turning the lights out in a room, distractants correspond to turning them up so high that we can't see anything else; the harmful effects of distractants are much the same as those of drugs.

Nearly any source of pleasure may be used as a distractant. Watching television can distract people from knowing that they can't stand each other; driving fast can distract us from knowing that we're afraid to ask for a raise; and having children has sometimes been used as a technique for hiding the fact that people have made a mistake in their marriage choice. Distractants can be as dangerous as drugs.

12. Don't expect your chief pleasures to come only at times or in places the culture deems pleasurable.

Meeting a friend on a street corner may be more exhilarating than blowing a horn on New Year's Eve. If it is to you, meet more friends and de-emphasize the blowing of horns. Don't let anyone, including those dearest to you, tell you which people or activities you *ought* to enjoy, or when you ought to enjoy them.

For many people New Year's Eve is a time of great depression. There is a New Year's Eve syndrome in the United States, which includes feeling isolated, sad, and undesirable. Those who suffer from it usually hold the mistaken belief that everyone else is enjoying the occasion and that they alone are not with loved ones. If you don't have the feelings expected of you at weddings, funerals, or birthdays, don't pretend to yourself that you do, or you'll lose your ability to identify what your true feelings are. There's only one way to stay in touch with your feelings and that is to make your own judgments about them, for better or for worse.

13. Examine yourself for prudery about affection.

Our era is prudish about affection. Many people find it harder to admit that they love a parent than that they want to take advantage of someone. They reserve their affection for children, where they excuse it by saying that children need affection, and for their husbands and wives, where they can safely regard their affectionate acts as sexual. Moreover, the misconception has sprung up that feelings prevent us from thinking clearly; and the premium these days is on intelligence.

14. Interpret your own surprise and disappointment.

As a student I once expressed great disappointment at an instructor's failure to nominate me for a fellowship which I deserved and for which I was nominated by all the other professors. When I told a friend that I was surprised at what I considered the instructor's betrayal of me, he reminded me that I'd already told him I thought the instructor disliked me. He said that if I was surprised, I must have disbelieved what I'd been saying, or that at the very least, I must have entertained the thought that I might be wrong and that the instructor respected my ability. Before he had voted against me, I would surely have denied possessing so much as the hope that he would vote in my favor. However, I must have nurtured that hope. I can infer that fact from my disappointment. Whereas the hope did not sneak past the censor of my consciousness, the disappointment did.

Since then I've listened to many patients describing their parents and bosses in ways that should have led them to expect the very treatment they later received, and yet they were surprised or disappointed at it. Obviously, they hadn't fully believed their own assertions.

Surprise and disappointment can be very useful cues to attitudes we've held. Because they are sudden and acute reactions, they often manage to burst through to consciousness, whereas the underlying attitudes they betray do not. Stop for a moment when you're surprised or disappointed, and ask yourself why. Very often you'll discover some attitude you've held, which you have either not identified or not acknowledged. Discrepancy is the key to discovery. This is an important principle of science. Moments of surprise, if you examine them, can lead you to important discoveries about yourself.

15. Try to be alert to other people's feelings.

When another person describes a feeling to you, especially if it is strong and he is beseeching you to listen, don't answer him by recommending some course of action for him to take. It may be far more important to him to know that you understand how he feels—frustrated, enraged, or hopelessly in love—than to hear your advice about what he should do. Many of us find it hard to communicate feelings, and we do so only occasionally and indirectly. When someone close to you talks about a feeling, consider the possibility that he wants mainly to convey to you how he feels; any answer used in place of a simple communication that you appreciate what he is saying is very likely to be perceived as dismissal. If you stay on the alert to how other people feel, and attentive to conveying that you are catching emotional tones in conversations, you will heighten your awareness of your own feelings.

CHAPTER 3

The Necessary Starting Place for Self-Help

IN THE NINETEENTH century two sets of James brothers became famous in this country. In the West, Jesse and Frank rose from humble origin to become our most celebrated train robbers; in New England, Henry and William became two of our most prominent intellectuals. Henry, whose writings are translated into every modern language, was a major American novelist. William ranks, without question, as America's foremost philosopher and psychologist; and unless someone as dashing as Tyrone Power comes along and plays Jesse again, William will probably remain even more famous than Jesse is. A sizable fraction of professional psychologists in the United States consider William a more significant contributor to psychology than Freud. I don't want to enter the controversy, but I do want to get attention for the quote from William James that I'm about to present. Over the last ten years I've thought about its implications nearly every day.

"Action seems to follow feeling, but really action

and feeling go together, and by regulating the action, which is under the more direct control of the will, we can indirectly regulate the feeling, which is not."

I want to discuss two implications of this statement. The first is that we must not hold ourselves directly accountable for our emotions, in the sense of considering ourselves better or worse people because of particular ones. Since feelings are not under the direct control of the will, we must try to judge ourselves by how we act, not by how we feel. This conclusion needs little said about it. The second is that the best levers for therapy are our own actions. The development of a therapy method which allows us to change our psyches by making enlightened choices of *action* is to be the main subject matter of this book.

Let's begin with the first issue, that of exempting ourselves from self-judgments based on our thoughts, attitudes, and feelings, which may be involuntary.

Whoever you are, you have a personal orientation, a complex set of feelings, attitudes, and beliefs, which are relatively constant. Your past actions have done a great deal to produce the pattern of thoughts and attitudes which now characterizes you. However, now that it's here, you can't wish it away: you've got to undertake new modes of action to change it. There's no sense blaming yourself for fear of authorities, or for the fact that you can't enjoy sex, or that you're lacking in confidence. If you blame yourself for anything, it must be for actions, since you can control them.

Many people blame themselves for what they cannot control so as to divert attention from activities which they know would help them but which they don't want to undertake.

Harry eats when he's anxious, which is much of the time, and when he's not eating, he loathes himself for being fat. In our first session he whimpers that he's useless to anyone, and thereby exempts himself from the feeling that he'll be doing himself further harm by overeating. I question him about what he eats but he doesn't like talking about the specifics of how he takes in more than eleven thousand calories a day.

During the ten minutes after he leaves my office, his being fat won't be a matter of choice, but his eating will. I've just made a very simple distinction—between what is voluntary and what is not, but the stress on where he can emphasize choice isn't of interest to Harry. He berates himself for obesity, as though the obesity were a choice, and that way his eating bothers him less.

It ought to be universally accepted that there's no sense berating yourself for the *consequence* of a choice, or for anything that you can't control. Direct your attention to what you can help. If you're afraid of your boss, don't berate yourself for the fear; though like obesity, fear may be a consequence of choices you have been making. If doing a slipshod job while the boss was away made you frightened of him, blaming yourself for the fear won't help, whereas blaming yourself for taking advantage of him is one of many steps you can take toward becoming less afraid.

Here are some ways to help you accept your feelings without condemning yourself for them. First, never belittle other people for their emotional reactions, no matter what they are; and if they talk about being angry or annoyed with someone, don't make the mistake of concluding that they necessarily dislike the person.

The second is, hold yourself accountable for all your decisions. If you ascribe your choices to powerful passions, you may find relief from guilt this time; however, the feelings you vilify will return, and having attributed to them power over you, you will fear them more in the future. Accepting responsibility for everything you do goes hand in hand with enjoying exemption from guilt over feelings, and thus responsibility is the stepping stone to personal freedom.

Finally, accept the fact that other people—even people insignificant in your life—have the power to induce feelings in you. Since a nagging wife may arouse in her husband desire to seek affection from someone else, it seems unfair for the husband to pay the double penalty of being nagged and also feeling loathsome because of his desire. Acknowledge that your feelings are not always under control and you'll free yourself from much of your guilt over having them.

CHAPTER 4

The Action Approach

OUR PERSONAL ORIENTATION is relatively stable by the time we become adult; we are conscious of only part of it. It is made up of all the long-standing beliefs that have emotional meaning to us. This orientation has been called in recent years our character structure—a term that William James did not use; however, he has told us in effect that by undertaking new modes of activity, we can alter our character structure.

If James is correct, what we need is knowledge of how the various behavior patterns that we may possibly undertake will influence us. Such knowledge would enable each of us to find the particular courses of action that would reshape our character structure according to our needs—for instance, rid us of anxiety, or fear of authorities, or guilt.

However, after stating that there is leverage for changing our underlying attitudes in activities that we ourselves can undertake, James leaves us struggling on the road. He doesn't give us a set of principles that would enable us to identify the actions with power to alter our character structure. All he does is to suggest a procedure so simple that most of us have tried it already and found it to have limited use or to fail completely. William James tells us simply to act like the people we want to become and promises us that if we do so faithfully, we shall turn ourselves into precisely those people.

Here are his words. I've included the paragraph already given and the advice that follows.

"Action seems to follow feeling, but really action and feeling go together, and by regulating the action, which is under the more direct control of the will, we can indirectly regulate the feeling, which is not.

"Thus the sovereign path to cheerfulness, if our cheerfulness be lost, is to sit up cheerfully and to act and speak as if our cheerfulness were already there."

The discovery that this very simple advice is useless to the vast majority of sufferers leaves open two logical possibilities. One is that our actions do *not* reach deeply enough inside us to alter our character structure. The other is that they do but that a much more complicated procedure must be followed for us to bring to bear sufficient power to alter it.

During the first half of the twentieth century, the majority of psychotherapists assumed the truth of the first of these alternatives, largely because of the influence of Sigmund Freud. Freud believed that no matter how wisely we choose our actions, and regardless of the order in which we choose them, we do not as individuals have sufficient power to rearrange our own character structure once the era of childhood is passed. Since most psychotherapists who have given their attention to the problem of personality change have been disciples of Freud, the conclusion that by the time we are adult we are helpless to bring about permanent change in our character structure has been the prevailing one. Though psychoanalysts of different schools have disagreed with Freud about how character structure forms and what has to _be_ done to change it, there has been agreement among them that new choices alone do not give a person sufficient leverage to alter his character structure.

Psychoanalysts have taught us an immense amount about personality and have enriched us with observations, but Freud's therapy process and later variants of it have not fulfilled the promises that were made for them. Though hopefulness about the possibility of accomplishing personality change has increased in recent years, belief in psychoanalysis appears to be on the wane. A group of psychotherapists who had been working in obscurity, the behavioral therapists, are becoming more prominent. As their name suggests, they argue that new choices of behavior are sufficient to rearrange our character structure, so that the power is, after all, in the hands of the individual, despite the fact that he is very likely to *feel* helpless and to report a character structure which has remained largely unchanged and which seems to resist the best efforts he can muster to change it.

Freud made many observations that led him to discount the possibility that any kind of action therapy could work. Chief among them was that there seems to be a formation of character structure early in life and that childhood experiences tend to be more influential than later ones. This meant that as we grow older, our pattern of attitudes assumes a stable form and it becomes increasingly difficult for us to change. Freud showed us that we are even more consistent as individuals than had previously been thought. He showed us that to some degree each of us perceives himself in ways he learned to perceive himself as a child, and perceives other people as similar to his parents and others important in his early life. Even when we feel surest that we are varying from our accustomed ways, we are often responding to the dictates of unconscious motivations and executing the demands of our character structure. It was pointed out to us that our attempts to alter our character structure by new modes of action often result in anxiety, and that even our sternest efforts to change frequently end in failure. From the fact that we are more consistent than had been thought and that our usual attempts to reshape our character structure by adopting new modes of action are failures, Freud and his disciples were ready to conclude that *all* approaches based upon adopting new activities must fail. However, there is no reason to draw this conclusion, as we shall see.

I'm going to present some principles, each indicating a route by which our actions affect our character structure. If we are to master a technique of changing ourselves by actions, we must understand how these principles operate. These principles may operate simultaneously when we act, sometimes causing single decisions to produce a diversity of effects on us, effects which we may learn to distinguish, and even predict. Ordinarily, we pay attention to some of these effects, but not the others. The effects most apt to go unobserved are often the most significant ones, and thus the principles that direct our attention to these effects are extremely important.

Examining each of these principles singly is necessary for understanding how they work. I should like to begin by illustrating their operation in contexts where the effects they predict are easiest to see. They reveal that our own behavior exerts a profounder influence on us than is usually believed; they account for much of the data that Freud observed; and most important, they can help us plan courses of action which when we follow them produce lasting changes in our personality.

CHAPTER 5

The Interaction and the Vantage-Point Effects

ONE ROUTE BY which our actions eventually influence our own thoughts is indirect. What we do influences people's opinions of us; and from their reactions to our behavior we draw some part of our opinion of ourselves. A braggart antagonizes people, causing them to withdraw from him. From their reactions he comes to feel that he is inadequate and that people are almost impossible to impress. Believing himself unnoticed and unheard, he invents stories of accomplishments even grander than those he has talked about in the past—a tactic which antagonizes people further, provoking reactions that in the end make him feel even less desirable. His bragging is, by its influence on other people, producing an eventual change in his own attitude toward himself. Changes of this sort follow what we may call the interaction route; it seems meaningful to say that he is producing an *interaction effect* on himself.

Mastering interaction effects is a matter mainly of learning how people respond to different sorts of treatment and of developing techniques for dealing with them. The most celebrated writer on the subject in our lifetime was Dale Carnegie, whose book *How to Win Friends and Influence People* is still widely read, twenty-five years after its publication. I often recommend the book to patients who make unnecessary difficulties for themselves in relationships. But though there is obvious value in knowing how people react and in learning how to minister to their needs, many of us overestimate the rewards that winning friendships will provide us with. We design life strategies to win good opinions, as though we needed these opinions to form good opinions about ourselves, when we ought to see plainly that the value of other people's liking us and even loving us is limited. We all know of instances in which the esteem of millions has failed to satisfy someone's yearning to feel important. We know there are people with apparently everything to live for who feel worthless and demoralized, and that some such people have even committed suicide. Where our purpose is to heighten our self-esteem, courting other people's esteem is taking a devious and uncertain route, uncertain because it cannot give us our anticipated result unless other people react precisely as we want them to.

Our actions exert a second kind of effect on us, less obvious but at least as important as the interaction effect. They supply us with the "vantage point" from which we observe other people's behavior. Did you ever play hooky from school and then see a friend of your father standing outside the movie theater as you went in? How did you feel about him? Did he look like a spy? And were you happy to see him when he came to your house that night? If you weren't, the reason is almost certainly that your own behavior had influenced your perception of him. The change in your attitude toward him could not have been due to an interaction. He may not even have seen you.

Consider this instance in which the second effect—which I shall call the *vantage-point effect*—was present. At a cocktail party I found myself sitting next to a handsome young man who confided in me that all the girls present were boring; they were there only to find someone to marry.

"You mean none of them really enjoys being here?" I asked.

"You know the group they're from," he said. I didn't and he went on to tell me that they were there only to find a man who was socially acceptable and making a good living. He lowered his voice slightly as though we were in a conspiracy. I enjoyed the fantasy for a moment that maybe we were going to kill Julius Caesar, but what it really amounted to was that we needed our combined intelligence to combat that of the merciless women who would trick us into marrying one of their number and burden us with working for them until someday we fell dead of exhaustion.

How did this young man, an accountant, come to so sweeping a conclusion? He was at the same party I was. And why did he trust me? For all he knew, I was on the side of the girls and was there to help draw him into their clutches. Apparently, the fact that I was a man was enough to win his trust. There was a powerful bias in his perceptions, a bias that, luckily, most of the other people at the party didn't share. As it turned out, this young man, named Neil, had been generating this same warped perception for years. At the party I was privileged to be able to watch him in action producing and reproducing his bias.

When Neil had entered the room he found a group of young men and women discussing the lead book review in that morning's *Sunday Times*. The discussion had turned to how much money the book might earn and Neil had made an estimate, adding that he was an accountant with a firm that handled many best-selling books. With that statement he enticed a girl into asking him where he worked. One question led to another and within the next five minutes he made it known that he was already a junior partner in his firm and that his future was very bright. The little group in which he and I were standing dissolved but not before Neil had won the interest of several girls.

But notice what Neil did to himself. He had come to the party with the belief that all the girls there would be ambitious and parasitic, and he had dealt with them accordingly. By implicitly promising a successful future to each new girl he met, he made it impossible for himself to discover whether this belief was false. Girls who liked him necessarily appeared to be in pursuit of the security and social status he offered, and that included girls who liked him in spite of his bragging and not because he appeared prosperous. Those who disliked him withdrew from him without telling him what was wrong; and regarding them Neil concluded that he had failed because he had not projected a future promising enough. Thus his own behavior doomed him to retain the picture of women and of himself that he had started with.

Neil went to many parties, as he told me later on, and wherever he went, he said, the story was the same. The women who gave him their telephone numbers did so only because he looked like the perfect provider.

"Do you think that all women have the same problem?" I asked. He answered, No, that perhaps he himself was lacking in appeal.

I looked at him and he was smirking. "Perhaps," I said, pretending to take him seriously.

And then, to my surprise, he said he'd been thinking about that possibility. I wanted to drop the subject but when he pressed me further, I told him I thought he harbored a distrust of all women and was paying the price for it.

Neil doubtless antagonized some people, but the chief way in which his actions harmed him was that they biased his own perceptions, perpetuating his pessimism about women and what they wanted. By his behavior he had made it impossible for himself to recognize that he was desirable to certain women and had no need to brag to them. Neil's pessimism about women was not a reaction to how they had behaved toward him but to how he had behaved toward them; thus his attitude toward women could not be altered by new behavior on their part. Nothing except new behavior by Neil could change it. Not an interaction effect, but the effect of holding to a vantage point was at the heart of his difficulty.

Our actions, whatever they are, provide us with many and complex vantage points, and for the most part, they hold us at those vantage points. Since they cause many of our ills by doing so, we ought often to consider the vantage-point effects of our actions, as well as their interaction effects.

If Neil had harmed himself by causing people to dislike him instead of by suppressing evidence that he was likable, he would have been more likely to see what the trouble was. As he lay in his tub on a Saturday night and mulled over why he didn't get invited somewhere, he might conceivably have reconsidered whatever behavior had harmed him. We're more likely to correct behavior that other people might object to than we are to change activities that appear to be winning approval, or at least not losing it. Strictly speaking, everything we do contributes to our vantage point, since if we had acted otherwise we would have given ourselves a different vantage point, and at least some of the observations we made would have allowed different interpretations.

Vantage-point effects play significant roles in cases of prejudice. If you believe that blacks are thieves and you lock your valuables in a closet on Wednesdays, when the black maid comes to clean (this is precisely the story a patient told me not long ago), then nothing the black maid ever does or can do, can convince you that your evaluation of her is wrong. Presumably, if you are careful to hide your maneuver (as the patient who told me the story was), you'll remove your valuables an hour before she comes. She won't discover what you have done, and you won't discover that what you've done was unnecessary. Once you've begun to act on the premise that she would steal if given the chance, you have inclined yourself to go on taking measures to stop her from stealing from you—measures which suppress the evidence that might have led you to abandon your premise.

The patient who told me that she removed her jewelry tried to defend her act by saying that the cost of the measure was slight. However, among the penalties she paid was that she reduced the amount of trust she felt she could put in the maid, and as a result, always felt somewhat uncomfortable when in her presence. It is impossible to take a measure against being harmed without putting a governor on the degree of comfort one can feel in the presence of the person against whom the measure is taken. The vantage-point principle tells us one reason why. By hiding her valuables every week, the woman contributed to her feeling that colored people are essentially different from whites—different in their attitude toward jewelry that they find in someone else's home.

In connection with the vantage-point effect, it is helpful to introduce the concept of the *needless maneuver,* the unnecessary defensive act that stops us from seeing what the world would be like if we had resisted the impulse to make this maneuver. Harmful vantage points are very often the result of needless maneuvers, as with Neil and the woman who hid her valuables. Needless maneuvers are much worse than wastes of time; they deprive us of information, and sometimes of information that would be very important for us to have.

Needless maneuvers are usually found where there are prejudices, and learning how to detect them may be a necessary first step toward relieving yourself of a prejudice. What are the fraudulent premises that you act on and the needless maneuvers that renew your belief in them? Do you use needless maneuvers such as being more courteous to people with wealth and social leverage than toward people poorer than you? If so, you are renewing your belief that wealth ought to entitle one to preferential treatment, and are making your own economic status seem unduly important. You can apply the question wherever you think it is relevant.

So far I've discussed two ways in which our actions affect us: by the *interaction effect,* and by providing us with a *vantage point* which necessarily influences how we interpret many of our observations. By producing a steady stream of both of these effects, our behavior influences our view of ourselves and other people more than most people realize; and thus, even considering these two effects without the two to be mentioned, we see that we have at least some power to influence our attitudes and our perceptions by our behavior.

CHAPTER 6

Direct Effect

THE THIRD PRINCIPLE explaining how our actions affect our subsequent attitudes is the most important. I'll call it the principle of *direct effect*. We produce direct effects whenever we act. It is mainly because of direct effects that, if we plan our strategies carefully, it is possible for us to use our actions to turn ourselves into the people we want to be.

The direct-effect principle explains, among other things, why William James's suggestion sometimes works and why it sometimes fails. The principle is that whenever we make a decision, we are, for a time, intensifying whichever attitudes gave rise to the decision in proportion to the contributions they have made. This effect is usually blocked from our awareness by the opposite reaction, immediate relief from the impulse, which occurs the instant after we act. One need only consider direct effects for a few days to appreciate the implication of the principle—that our actions produce far more sweeping effects on our underlying attitudes than is usually believed.

Nearly every decision has multiple motivations, and therefore the principle implies that a single act exerts effects on many of our already held attitudes. As a rule, most of these attitudes are not conscious, and thus relatively few of the direct effects on us of our actions are apparent. As will be shown later, we can even use the principle of direct effect to identify motivations for acts already carried out. Some practice at seeing the principle in operation is needed before using it to help us account for more complicated phenomena.

First, consider the problem of why two people acting identically may affect themselves very differently.

An employee likes his boss who has been kind to him, and in a sudden spirit of warmth he decides to give his boss a box of cigars. Late on Friday afternoon he leaves a short note together with the box on his boss's desk and goes home; as he rides on the train he feels happy and likes the boss even more than he did. Another employee, who feels he is on the verge of being fired because the boss dislikes him, also leaves a box of cigars on the boss's desk, but his motive for leaving them there is to secure his status on the job—a status which he feels may already be lost. Whereas the first employee has increased his fondness of the boss by giving him the cigars, the second has not. As he rides on the train he has no warm feelings for the boss. His gift has, if anything, increased his dislike of the boss and concern over losing his job.

Similar acts have exerted two very different effects, and the reason for the difference is that the *motivations* for the two acts were different. However, one thing can be said about both acts. Each of them intensified the particular motivation for it.

The main reason that an act carried out identically can affect different people differently, or even the same person differently at different times, is that the *motivations* for the act are likely to be different, and careful analysis shows that among their other effects all our acts tend to intensify the motivations for them. I've deliberately chosen a comparison in which the boss himself did not interact with either of the two employees, so that no reaction of his could have influenced either one. The reactions of other people to our behavior are usually what we look at first, and so the operation of the direct-effect principle on us is less likely to be perceived when interactions occur than when they don't; however, this is not to say that the principle ceases to operate or becomes any less important when we are interacting with people than when we are alone.

According to the direct-effect principle, if the feelings that lead us to act include love of somebody, then our particular act intensifies the love—whether or not subsequent interactions with that person, or reflections about him, influence us otherwise. If fear is a motivation for an act, the act intensifies that fear—whether or not the immediate relief we feel in removing ourselves from a threat stops us from seeing that we've made ourselves more afraid of it. If hatred of someone motivates an act toward him, the act intensifies our hatred of him—whether or not we stop hating him for the moment because we've just spit out our venom at him. The direct effect of disliking him more, like the direct effects in the other cases, may be obscured from the actor by other elements of his experience, more immediate and apparent. However, direct effects occur whenever we act, since all our acts are motivated.

I want to continue with some examples in which interactions are absent before introducing some necessary complications. A young man is alone in his room; he considers it very important that he study hard in the next few hours because he has a test on the following day for which he is ill prepared. He has been dating a girl named Lily for three months, but tonight he is worried that she likes him less than she did and may be out on a date with someone else. While trying to study, he is interrupted several times by thoughts about her. To assure himself that she is home and that she hasn't given him up entirely, he decides to telephone her. He does and gets a busy signal. He realizes that one of her parents may have been on the phone, but even so he has intensified the worry that led him to dial her number. He has *by calling* increased his fear that she has no interest in him and is chatting with some new boyfriend. Moreover, he has intensified all the attitudes which, combined, contributed to his calling her. By the very act of dialing her number, he has, ever so slightly, increased his feeling that he is unworthy of her, and that she is already planning to end her relationship with him as painlessly as possible.

For the sake of discussion, I've presupposed that he didn't reach her on the phone. If he had, and she had responded warmly, she might possibly have melted his fear. But even in that case, though the increase in fear caused by his calling would have been compensated for, other of his motives—for instance, the belief that she was precious in his life—would have remained intensified as a result of his calling. Having heightened his fear by calling, the boy would have predisposed himself to misconstrue vagueness from her as evidence of rejection. If after getting a busy signal many times he had finally gotten her on the phone, his worry might have already grown so great that even her most reassuring statements could not have assuaged it.

Suppose instead that he had no fear of losing the girl, and that his main motivation for calling her was to postpone studying for his test in French to be given the next day, for which he felt inadequately prepared. This time his calling would not increase his fear of losing the girl. Dialing her number might have no effect on his view of her. However, because his motives included the belief that his work was burdensome, his calling would make the work seem harder once he went back to it; and if fear that the test was going to be difficult had been a motive, it would, ever so slightly, increase that fear.

Put off a task and you'll intensify whatever beliefs led you to put it off; you'll make yourself feel even more inadequate to the task and the task seem harder than it did. In putting off a task we see one of the purer cases in which direct effects are discernible. We ourselves are making a decision, and other people are not interacting with us at the time. Interestingly, there isn't an explanation that I can find in all psychoanalytic literature for the easily observable fact that putting off a task can change our attitudes toward ourselves and make the task look harder to us. I think the reason is that until recently, the almost invariable approach of psychoanalysis was to study behavior purely in terms of its motives, and seldom to consider the possibility that our actions influence our subsequent motives.

Let's look at a different kind of instance, still a relatively uncomplicated one. A man feels inadequate because he isn't a college graduate and he pretends to his friends that he is. His lying to them, which is motivated by the belief that it is discrediting to be poorly educated, is one of many activities by which he regenerates that belief over a long time period (and, in addition, the lying prevents him from discovering which of his friends would have regarded him as highly even if they knew precisely how many years of schooling he had completed). His corporation goes into bankruptcy and for a time he is without a job.

A job interview is scheduled for him by a friend, and as the time of the interview grows near he becomes increasingly frightened. On the one hand, he feels qualified for the job; on the other, he feels that his not being a college graduate makes him unqualified for it and that the interviewer will refuse to recommend him for it. He even imagines that the interviewer will consider him audacious in applying for a job for which he is unqualified.

If he allows the belief that he doesn't deserve the job to motivate him to avoid the interview, then his choice to stay home must necessarily intensify that belief, as well as the belief that the interviewer would consider him audacious were he to try for the job. As a result of his staying home he would feel less adequate and believe more strongly than ever that because he did not have a college degree he did not deserve the job.

He is likely to suffer more as a consequence of staying home than he would suffer if he had gone to the interview and had been rejected, since by going he would have increased his feeling that he deserved to be a candidate for the job; and with this belief, the interviewer's reaction would have been less significant than the imagined reaction of the interviewer. The penalty for defaulting is often greater than even the worst distress that a person might suffer if he had not succumbed to the impulse to avoid an encounter.

Notice that if the man were Negro and hadn't applied for the job because he believed that the interviewer would consider him unsatisfactory on that account, his choice to stay home would intensify that belief and might contribute to hatred of interviewers, and perhaps to hatred of all whites who are in a position to give jobs to Negroes. If in addition to assuming that the interviewer was hostile, he entertained the thought that he was actually inferior because he was a Negro (having been told many times that this was so), then he would, by defaulting, have intensified his conviction that he was actually inferior. Any act motivated by the belief that one is inferior because of some particular trait intensifies that belief.

Henry Ford once said that a man will never forgive you for the wrongs he has done to you. There is great truth in this statement, though it may be an exaggeration; and the main reason is that our treatment of anyone tends to intensify the attitudes motivating it. One corollary is, Treat people with kindness if you would continue to respect them and enjoy their company. Another is, Be careful not to allow people to mistreat you even if they love you. Their mistreatment, though it may not harm you at the time, may well intensify their disdain for you: in many cases, by their mistreatment they predispose themselves to think less of you and treat you worse in the future. Many parents of our generation are now paying the price for their permissiveness, for having allowed their children to treat them disdainfully and thereby generate disdain for them. If you want to preserve the respect of people who love you, stop them if you can, from acting in ways that will destroy their respect for you.

Let's look back at the William James statement

now, that acting cheerfully is the sovereign path to feeling cheerful. I want to present a noteworthy exception to the rule, which is explained by the direct-effect principle.

A patient came into my office and described himself as feeling "filthy inside." He didn't know why and said he had been happy when he got up that morning. He and his wife had been quarreling in recent weeks but a few days earlier they had made up and were now enjoying a pleasant relationship. He was a highly principled man, who had worked as a television director for a major network and had recently changed his job to that of producing a show. He had spent the earlier part of that afternoon with three executives from the company that sponsored the show. Previously, in his capacity as director he had known them only vaguely but now his association with them was closer. This was the second time he had eaten lunch with them and he had come to my office straight from a lavish restaurant where he had spent several hours with them.

One of the men had talked about extramarital affairs and had suggested arranging some dates for Bill, my patient, when the show would be filmed in Florida. Bill had said no, he wasn't interested. Later on, the man had talked about raising the expense budget of the show in order to pocket extra money from the sponsor; according to this man and the others, all of them would profit, including Bill. Bill had said nothing to this, but he told me he would sooner leave his job than accept a dime of dishonest money, and he didn't know what to do. As we talked, it became clear that Bill felt disgust, not because of anything the three men had said but because he had lunched with them and had chosen not to take a stand when they had tried to persuade him to violate principles in which he believed. What bothered him most, he said, was the fact that he had acted so *cheerfully* while he was with them; he had talked and laughed with them very much as he had with his wife recently, while they were happy together; and in view of their offers of women, he felt like a traitor to her.

Acting cheerfully certainly didn't cheer him up, and in fact his choice to act cheerful with people he despised was the main reason for his disgust. After long talks with his wife about his work, he left the job of producer to direct another television show where the salary was slightly less but he could act according to his own ethics. The reason that acting cheerfully didn't prove the sovereign path to cheerfulness for Bill was that his motivations did not include underlying cheerfulness.

By the same logic, because our motivations are important in determining the effects on us of our actions, aggressive actions don't always produce rage, and running away from someone does not always make us more afraid of him.

Notice the relevance of motivation in the following contrast between two cases. Many of the Jews who lived in Europe during the Second World War denied being Jewish to save their lives. Doing so certainly didn't make them ashamed of being Jewish; if anything, these people became more fervently religious than Jews who lived in countries without pogroms. Where the desire to preserve their Jewish culture was part of their motivation for trying to outwit their persecutors, their subterfuge heightened their belief that their culture was worth preserving. Force a man to fight for an issue, and if he manages to survive, he'll believe in that issue more strongly than he did.

On the other hand, the Jewish resident of a city like New York who changes his name and lies to get into a posh athletic club which he thinks might refuse to accept a Jew, affects himself differently. This time, where the motives include a sense of disgrace over being Jewish, changing his name and lying increase that sense of disgrace. His lying intensifies his belief that getting into the club is important and that the other members would discriminate against a Jew. After lying to them, as he sits in their company he must necessarily feel that he and other Jews have something to hide and that the club members' disdain for Jews is warranted. The price he pays in demoralization is apt to be worse than the worst effects of harassment which the other members could have visited on him. The direct effects of our actions are often more potent than the effects on us of other people's treatment of us, and in fact, as we have seen, our own behavior plays a major role in determining how we interpret other people's behavior.

Not just direct effects but vantage-point effects are usually significant in cases like this last one. If the club members were not really anti-Semitic, the person who denied being Jewish would have allowed himself no chance of discovering that fact. It is often helpful to separate the different effects on us of our actions. The eventual influence on us of nearly any act may be a combination of two of the effects mentioned, or of all of them. Vantage-point effects stop us from discovering evidence that might lead us to change our beliefs. However, where we have intensified a belief, direct effects have nearly always played a more prominent role.

CHAPTER 7

The Process of Change

MOST ATTITUDES OF concern to us underlie many of our activities. For instance, if a girl dreads sexual contact with men, that dread is almost sure to be motivating more activities than mere avoidance of sexual contacts. Very likely, it is playing some part in determining her choices of friends, and decisions she makes in decorating her apartment, in choosing clothing, and in buying records. As we grow older, most of our attitudes come to motivate a widening sweep of activities. This is nearly always true where the attitude in question is dread of sexual contact. More generally, it is safe to say of nearly any purely personal attitude that if we have held it for a long time period, we are unknowingly reproducing it, or holding it in place, not by a single activity but by a multiplicity of them.

It follows from this that we can seldom alter attitudes by adopting single practices, or by stopping them. Our character structure, which is a complex pattern of interlocking attitudes, allows change of any of its component parts. But to change any part—e.g., to get rid of any specific fear or dread, we must identify *much* of the behavior renewing that part, and discontinue it.

A young man tells me that he suffers what seems to him an insurmountable fear of authorities. He describes himself as incapable of making even simple requests of them. Here too, we may say with near certainty, even before pursuing the matter, that the fear is being held in place not by some single activity but by many of them.

Each of these people reports feeling helpless to get rid of a seemingly insurmountable fear. The young man may tell me that at different times he has tried to confront his boss but has become embarrassed, has been at a loss for words, and has skulked away. The woman may report having tried to force herself through a sexual act and having become petrified, with the result that she now feels incapable of going ahead with it. Both feel helpless because they have already tried to change their underlying attitude and failed. However, the reason each has failed is that the attempt to change the attitude has consisted merely of his going into the teeth of it—that is, making a local attack by behaving as though the attitude didn't exist. While each of these people was fighting his local skirmish, he was unknowingly renewing the unwanted attitude by other behavior; in effect, he was arming the enemy while doing battle with it on its strongest front. When finally he gave up his battle in despair, he concluded that he was helpless to defeat the unwanted attitude and that his character structure was fixed and had him in thrall.

During the period that each was professing his helplessness, they were each unknowingly reinfecting themselves with their fear by a multitude of acts; the only way they could rid themselves of their fear would have been to identify that multitude of acts and change them systematically. In the next chapter I'll talk about how character structure develops; my intention now is only to indicate why it seems so firm to us, and to present a general outline of what we must do to change it. Naturally, no two people are identical in their behavior patterns, or in what their behavior means to them. This includes people whose problems appear identical.

It follows that getting rid of any unwanted attitude demands careful search for the activities by which we are renewing it. And since some activities are easier to change than others, it also follows that there are preferable orders in which we should change activities, orders by which we can relieve ourselves gradually of our particular fear and be certain of defcating it when we make our head-on attack.

Not understanding that a multitude of activities contribute to holding nearly any significant attitude in place, some therapists who are exponents of an action approach have advised their patients to do the very thing that the patient has already tried to do— that is, to make a head-on assault by acting in the face of the fear without first laying siege to it. For instance, girls with sexual problems like the one I described have sometimes been advised to force themselves to go to bed with someone "for practice," and frequently, after they've tried, on the premise that their therapist's confidence in them would give them the confidence they needed, they have found the experience even more distressing than their worst nightmares about it had been. Not only have these people often lost faith in their therapist as a result; many have reached the unfortunate conclusion that no mere sequence of actions, no matter how carefully charted, could guide them toward healthier attitudes and allow them to enjoy sexual experiences.

One girl who had reached that conclusion told me in our first session that she had recently condemned a friend for what she considered promiscuity and that she had ostracized a girl from her sorority for going to bed with several men. By both of these acts, and by others like them, she was making it harder for herself to enjoy sexual experiences. Apparently her therapist had overlooked the significance of this sort of behavior, perhaps because like many of us he was oriented to consider actions unimportant in revitalizing attitudes. With that orientation, he would regard such acts, if he paid attention to them at all, only as manifestations of the girl's problem and not as activities which if changed could help her solve the problem.

Not condemning other people is a good first step toward relieving the tension of unwanted attitudes.

When the girl allowed the ostracized friend to reenter her life, she discovered that spending time with the friend made her anxious. However, doing so eventually lessened her anxiety somewhat, and was a step toward reducing her embarrassment at the thought of a sexual contact. After making a sequence of changes, each of which readied her for others, she reported a gradual lessening of her fear; and finally, when she went to bed with her fiancé shortly before marrying him, she was surprised that the experience was not dreadful at all, though it did not become pleasurable for some time.

One of the most exciting parts of doing therapy (with other people and occasionally with myself) is discovering actions which, though they bore no apparent relevance to some problem of interest, were critical in reinfecting us with it. The combinations of motives that may give rise to any activity are unlimited; it is impossible, therefore, to determine with certainty the motivations for an act simply from knowing what the act was. For instance, arguing can be an expression of love or hate; belittling someone can be an attempt to win his approval, and often is, as when a child belittles a parent for not appreciating him or not being up to date. Since the connections between act and motive are so varied, the course of therapy often demands that we change activities whose motives we misunderstood or which we considered routine and which seemed to bear absolutely no relation to our problem. Sometimes we must carry out painstaking trial and error procedures to discover the behavior infecting us with a problem.

Think about the behavior which in this following case helped keep an unwanted attitude alive.

Someone I knew casually, who was driving me home from the country, told me his boss was a bully and asked me if I could suggest some tactics in dealing with him. I said I couldn't think of anything offhand, and he went on to tell me that he always had difficulty in making requests of his superiors and that he couldn't object when they made unfair demands of him.

While we were talking, a summer storm broke out, making visibility very bad. Many cars pulled over to the side of the road to wait it out. I told my friend that there was a gas station ahead and that we would do better stopping there. When we reached it, naturally the attendants were inside, but my friend seemed slightly annoyed. The rain was pelting the car and I didn't want to get out even to make a phone call.

"Where are the attendants?" my friend asked. He drove the car up alongside the pump, saying, "While I'm here I might as well get some gas."

Finally one of the attendants came out, an older man dressed in a raincoat with a hood that covered his head. My friend asked for a dollar's worth of gas. I could hardly believe that he would trouble someone with so little reason, since we were within a few miles of New York City and had enough gas to get to Canada. When my friend also suggested that perhaps the fellow ought to check the oil, I said, "Don't you think you're being a little tough on him?"

"What do you mean?" he said. "It's my right to get gas here."

"Yes, but if you notice, nobody else is exercising that right at this particular time," I said. "If you were in dire need of gas I could understand it. Why don't you give the fellow a break?"

My friend closed the window so as not to get wet while the attendant was working outside. He opened it for about three seconds while he handed him a five-dollar bill, and when he got the four dollars in return, complained under his breath that the money was wet. In his haste not to get wet during the interchange he shut the window so fast that he almost caught the attendant's hand in it. I thought I was watching an old Charlie Chaplin film caricaturing the abuses by the rich.

A strong motivation for my friend's mistreatment of the attendant was the firmly lodged idea that people who hold rank over others have the right to use it as they wish, and that any complaints which an employee makes, even objections to being treated unfairly, are insubordination. Presumably, his actions with the attendant were characteristic of many others renewing his belief that people with rank hold the privilege of acting inhumanely toward subordinates. His finding it hard to complain when he felt his boss treated him unfairly was one of the costs to him of holding that belief. Thus, by his own behavior he was continuously draining himself of the capacity for indignation when injustices were done to him.

Changing his manner of dealing with people whom he regarded as subordinates would doubtless have been a step toward enabling him to feel that he deserved better treatment from his boss. However, I must admit I was not inclined that day to lecture to him, perhaps because I was annoyed with him, or because I felt that whatever I said would be disregarded. I have intended merely to illustrate how an activity that seems at first glance to bear no relation to a problem may actually be part of a constellation of behavior which has been aggravating the problem by holding an unwanted attitude in place. Such activities are sometimes hard to discover—impossible to discover when we don't look for them; and thus it is no wonder that many of us feel helpless though the levers for personality change are in our hands.

In this chapter I have meant to make clear that not single acts but perseverance, with carefully thought out patterns of activities, is usually needed to produce personality change. The process demands constant rechecking of the effects of your actions and careful consideration of which activities ought to be undertaken next—procedures that demand knowledge of the principles given. Using the principles properly we can guide ourselves through highly intricate patterns of action which, when we pursue them, can produce changes in our psyches that we can make lasting and unmistakable.

CHAPTER 8

A Story from the Past

I WANT TO present a case illustrating the development of part of a person's character structure. In it, I think, are the answers to some important questions about how your character structure developed and why you may feel it is difficult to change.

Irene's father, a thickly muscled foreman in a cotton mill, married a woman devoted to him. The couple lived eight miles from the mill, in Connecticut, and Irene was their first child. She was ebullient and outgoing, resembling her mother closely, but her strongest recollections are of admiring her father. When she was very young he took her to his softball games, evenings and Sundays after church. Her earliest memory was of getting lost in thick underbrush during one of the games and of all the men looking for her and one of them finding her and picking her up and handing her over to her father who bore her on his shoulders to the custody of a woman sitting on one of the benches. Her feeling was that mankind's tumult of activity had stopped when she was lost, and everyone had come to look for her, out of respect for her father and out of desire to please him.

Her pleasure in being alive was connected in her mind with her father's physical strength, and she very much enjoyed being alive.

When she was five, a brother, Alan, was born. People swarmed to the house to visit her mother on her return from the hospital. Irene sought the company of her father's friends, who collected on the porch around a radio while the women were inside. But this time they paid no attention to her, and it was a nightmare in which she felt insignificant as they laughed among themselves and threw crushed beer cans into a wooden box and kidded about the athletic skill of Alan, as though he were already a man.

In the next few years the loss of favor rankled her and she turned to trial and error in attempting to regain her father's affection and interest in her. It seemed that just when she felt most abandoned, a second brother was born, confirming her fall from grace. Another boy. One might accidentally disappear, or run away, or die—but not two: Irene remembers that thought. She played pranks and tried to exhibit herself; she later rested her hopes on vigorous competitions with her brothers, but these failed since she discovered that superior accomplishments were expected of her. For a period she cried, wanting her father to pay more attention to her. But that tactic also failed. He looked surprised. After a time she came to think that her crying was foolish because that was how it appeared to him. She would detest herself for ever letting him see that she was hurt, as though she'd revealed a lofty and ludicrous hope. When on occasion he bent down and wiped away her tears, she drew back, sensing that his intention was only to pacify her and refusing to settle for anything less than the love he had formerly expressed.

The failure of all her trial and error methods thus far kept her in search of a pattern that would work for her. Then finally she found a route of access to her father. It was servitude.

She discovered that telling her parents when her brothers were out of bed, and putting them back when guests were there, pleased both her parents immensely. Tidying up her room and being polite were welcomed not just by her mother but by her father, who seemed to understand her now and smiled at her as he had when she was very young. Once again she was content. Within months she stopped feeling isolated and could even be concerned about her brothers. She was developing the attitude that it is important to be useful—and, connected with it, the implicit belief that she was worthless to people except when serving them.

During the years to come, she quite naturally allowed this attitude to influence her widening diversity of activities, enlarging upon her newly discovered role, which meant finding new and more subtle ways of making herself important to people. By the time she was twelve, she had made herself a highly consistent person, engaging in a complex meshwork of activities —all of which served to hold her character structure in place, and to give it an apparent rigidity. Among her more dominant attitudes was the confirmed belief that she would be undesirable unless she made herself useful to people.

You were born into a chaos too. You used trial and error. You found a pattern of attitudes that were acceptable, either because they won your parents' affection or because they allowed you to escape from your parents, or because they gratified you in some other way. You allowed those attitudes to motivate you. You widened the sweep of your activities, many of which reinstated this set of attitudes and locked them in place, and you continued enlarging on your behavior.

By the time Irene was in her teens, she was already suffering from the universal illusion of feeling as though she were inside herself and looking out, perceiving the world and not recognizing that her own actions were coloring her view. Think how farfetched it would have seemed to her if someone had told her that myriad acts, highly desirable from society's point of view, were in cumulation renewing her underlying sense that she was intrinsically worthless.

At twenty she fell in love with a boy named Arthur. Fear of losing him, and the conviction of her intrinsic worthlessness, motivated a multitude of decisions which seemed to her unmistakably called for. She tried never to disagree, or to complain or make demands. She willingly cooked for him nearly every night, typed his homework assignments for him; and she went so far as to ask him not to do things for her that he seemed eager to do. If she was really unworthy of him, complaining or expressing independent opinions would be dangerous; that was her logic. And thus by her own behavior she rapidly assigned to him the part of her father and to herself the part of the little child who had found a route of access and was still acting as if it were the only one.

The more she made herself useful to Arthur, the more intensely she felt that he would abandon her if she were not useful to him. She would lie awake nights going over her day's performances with him, wondering whether he loved her and asking herself repeatedly whether she'd done enough for him. As she increased her own burden, she lost her zest and became sullen when in his company.

Eventually Arthur decided to leave her. He gave her no advice that might veer her in another direction. Friends and lovers seldom give advice to people like Irene: when we like them, we don't want to risk hurting their feelings, they seem to be trying so hard; and finally, when we're forced to acknowledge to ourselves we've lost esteem for them, it appears to us that criticizing them will be futile, and instead we simply withdraw from them.

That summer she spent long hours telling herself his leaving her was unreal. She daydreamed about him continually, and even many years afterward she would sometimes dream about him at night and would wake up full of rage toward him for intruding into her life. Her saddest hours were those she spent alone when she scoured her own performance, recalling her dates with him and searching for ways she had failed to be the sort of person she imagined he wanted her to be. Irene had no way of interpreting the failure of any relationship she was in, except as an indication that she herself had been unable to make that relationship work. She vowed that she would do even more to please the next man she was to meet.

The vow made her easy prey for men who held her in contempt and were willing to exploit her. Her next boyfriend was such a man. During a brief affair with her he treated her shabbily and then suddenly stopped calling her. Irene felt too insignificant to allow herself the luxury of being angry with him. She recognized well that many girls drew kindlier treatment from men than she did, and without striving for it nearly so hard; and this recognition too seemed to confirm her suspicion that there was an intrinsic deficiency in her personality.

The feeling that her character structure had congealed and would be unchangeable was very strong when she came to me. She was convinced that she lacked some quality which made other women appealing to men and which she imagined she had possessed as a little girl and somehow lost. She wanted to get married, but was frightened of meeting someone eligible, believing that she would drive him away and corroborate her worst fears of her own inadequacy. She alternated between feeling abused by men and believing that they had all been well advised to leave her. She had been thinking about suicide. It distressed her that she was no longer attracted to men: she asked me if this meant she was a lesbian; she sobbed about having lost Arthur whom she still loved, and told me that he was married and that she knew exactly where he lived. She told me through tears that her case was hopeless, and repeated this so often that I came to feel she was undermining herself by the repetition. I pointed out to her that some part of her must have held out hope or she would not have come to me, and she agreed.

Therapy with her revealed a multiplicity of actions that were in effect duplicating the pattern which seemed to her to be frozen. She could not identify all the harmful behavior at once, much less change it; but there was a horizon of behavior that she could change immediately, and new practices enabled her to see further changes that were to be made, and to make them. For a time, when she was uncertain about her motivations in doing favors for people, she had to desist from doing them; after a while, when she had reduced her essential feelings of worthlessness, she was able to extend herself more, being certain this time that she was renewing warm feelings about people and not reinstating feelings of inadequacy.

Irene produced most of her cure within a year. It is a durable one: she is no longer goaded by the need to please other people excessively and takes pleasure in exercising her own abilities. From what I can gather, she is happily married. Like everyone, if she weren't aware of her motivations, she could conceivably intensify particular ones to disproportionate heights. There is no ultimate condition of stability that would guard us permanently against harming ourselves. Irene is now holding a different kind of character structure in place by a widening sweep of activities. The new pattern became firmly entrenched before we stopped working together. She is more aware of the dangers of excessive subservience than most of us, having suffered from overresponsiveness to the impulse. I would guess that if she has personality problems in the future, they will be of some other form, and not serious.

Our past affects us and sometimes very significantly, but not by rooting itself in our psyches so deeply that once we're adult we're helpless to root it out. It affects us in a different way—by presenting a context to us, a puzzle in early life, and inviting us to solve it as we can. Solving the puzzle means learning what our parents are like and what they want from us, and what capacities we have; and it also means learning how to act to secure the things we want. It means making whatever sense we can out of the chaos of early life and finding modes of activity that will provide us with love and gratifications.

It is as we solve the puzzle of early life and master the solutions we reach that we develop our identity—

the attitudes and feelings which appear to congeal but which in reality go on depending upon our behavior for their survival. As we repeat our behavior, building on what we learned and widening its diversity, we tend to renew our convictions about ourselves and to assign to people we meet the parts that our parents had. Thus the routes of access to our parents, which they allow us when we are young, are the primary coincidence of our lives, and we are the ones who unwittingly make them so.

CHAPTER 9

Trauma and What We Can Do about It

WE'VE ALWAYS KNOWN that events play a role in the shaping of character. But what gives an event the power to influence us? This question has been asked insistently in recent years, since Freud introduced the idea of trauma. Taking the word from biology where it means injury or wound, he applied it to what he called injuries to the psyche, and so a trauma came to mean an emotional experience or shock with a lasting psychological effect. Freud posed the question, Which experiences have the power to be traumatic? and, for a time, when psychoanalysis was in its infancy, Freud and his disciples believed that they would answer this question shortly.

However, because psychoanalysis didn't acknowledge the role of the individual in regenerating his own character structure, it was doomed from the start not to answer the question at all. The theory that character structure was some sort of stuff shaped by early experience led Freud and his followers to study the sorts of experiences that the infant and child are subjected to—as though experiences themselves were ultimately to be distinguished by their specific influences on psychic development. It wasn't long before psychoanalysts saw that even the most blatant sorts of events in peoples' lives did not have predictable influences on them. Some children of divorce made better adjustments than those who'd lived comfortably at home with both parents. Some children separated from their parents at birth were happy afterward and succeeded in forming relationships. Girls who were raped didn't always develop sexual problems, whereas other girls with no such experiences sometimes developed morbid sexual fears.

For years psychoanalysts held to the conviction that experiences themselves have power to be traumatic. They concluded that the events that are traumatic were more subtle than those they'd been looking at. An accidental comment a parent made, an observation the child made, or an impulse the child felt and then repressed, might be traumatic for him. Psychoanalysts never lacked in readiness to hypothesize, and the subject of trauma became a fruitful one for hypothesis. Schools of psychoanalysis developed around beliefs concerning which events were traumatic, and by the nineteen thirties one could be sure that if he went to psychoanalysts of five different schools, he would receive from each a different explanation of which events in his life had been traumatic for him.

Our understanding of trauma was even cloudier than it need have been because most of the evidence that led to the different theories was taken from people already adult. Patients lying on the couch would report episodes in their early lives, piecing together their recollections as well as they could; and the theories that psychoanalysts put in their books were constructed from these recollections. When the reading public, curious about the latest discoveries of psychoanalysis, got the idea that the experts believed that a single parental mistake might be traumatic for a child, there was much self-scrutiny and gingerly treatment of children. I think the era of "permissiveness" was stimulated by the fear that doing nearly anything would be wrong, a fear that derived in part from writings to the effect that we had more power to destroy our children than we had previously believed. Meanwhile there wasn't much good that parents could do. A trauma was a wound, and there wasn't a word in the psychoanalytic language meaning a stroke by a parent with beneficial effects. Though a theory explaining the growth of an attitude ought not have reference only to the growth of unwanted attitudes, the theory of trauma did. Clearly, the theory of trauma wasn't helping us predict anything, or control any part of our lives, better than in the past; and I think many of us felt relieved when Freud decided that it was a sequence of events and not a single event which was traumatic for the child in nearly every case. Parents would still have to be cautious, but at least they would no longer have to live in fear of making a single mistake.

A trauma is an event, or set of events, that causes a person to shift a behavior pattern, bringing some attitude into prominence. The attitude may be a response to the event, or may have predated it and become intensified by it. The attitude may be fear of something, or servility, or confidence, for example. There must be a change of behavior for an event to have lasting significance.

A girl of eleven is raped and afterward adopts a pattern of activity aimed at protecting her from men; she keeps her conversations with boys impersonal, doesn't talk about sexual intercourse and chooses as friends only girls who feel about sex as she does. By the time she comes to my office, she is renewing her repugnance by a highly intricate mode of activities. My getting her to talk about sexual intercourse is in effect peeling away one of those many activities, and she reports that doing so reduces her repugnance slightly. The rape, which started the change in her attitudes toward men, was certainly traumatic for her. But not in the sense that it damaged her pristine sexual eagerness and left her helpless to repair the damage done. It was traumatic in that it terrified her at the time and resulted in her adoption of behavior that continued to renew her fear.

Seeing her mother tremble and burst into tears when she told her about the rape was traumatic in much the same sense that the rape itself was. It was largely because of her mother's reaction that she vowed to be more careful in the future, and in the process regenerated her dread. It's hard to know whether the girl would have developed similar attitudes if she hadn't been attacked, since her mother might have frightened her into the pattern by telling her anecdotes about the dangers of men or by warning her constantly to stay away from men. On the other hand, if after the rape the mother had not added to the impact of the experience by expressing her own attitudes about it, the girl would have been less likely to develop dread. Thus both experiences, forming part of a constellation, were essential for the change.

Single events are rarely traumatic, by which I mean they're rarely sufficient to arouse in a person an attitude and start him on the track of renewing it. We become less susceptible to traumas as we grow older because most of our attitudes come to draw their sustenance from an increasing number of activities, making them increasingly sturdy against the onslaughts of new experiences.

Once we understand that everyday activities sustain our system of attitudes, trauma ceases to be a mystery. The most terrifying experiences may not be traumatic for us—and in fact, they positively cannot be, unless they induce us to change essential modes of behavior. If you, the parent, would stop a rape from becoming traumatic for your daughter, work as hard as you can at keeping her from changing her patterns of behavior after the episode. Since traumas always depend for their force on the person's changing behavior, there is much we can do to stop any experience from becoming traumatic for our children or for ourselves.

It's easy to see why psychoanalysts had trouble in identifying traumas; nearly any experience, or any sequence of experiences, can possibly be traumatic if the person is at a stage of readiness to act on the attitudes aroused in him. Our susceptibility is especially strong when we're learning new techniques. With sexual traumas, one can be too young as well as too old. The little girl who is seduced is less likely to regenerate dread of sex than the older girl who is on her way to learning how to talk to boys; and the woman of thirty-five, whose sexual attitudes rest firmly on practiced behavior, being unlikely to change that behavior, is the one most likely to preserve her orientation even after disastrous experiences.

What was the trauma in Irene's case? She turned from a volatile and pleasant little girl, interested in her own gratifications, into a sullen young adult, unappealing because she gave people the impression that life had dealt harshly with her and drained her of vitality. Obviously, the birth of her brothers had not in itself been enough to account for the transition. Her father's expectations of what a little girl should be like wouldn't have been enough either, since they might not have been manifested for many years if her brothers hadn't appeared on the scene to make them apparent. It took the combination of the birth of her brothers and the stereotyped expectations of her father, along with the particular abilities which Irene herself possessed, to cause her to regenerate her new set of attitudes about herself. Paradoxically, if her yearning for her father had been less intense, she might not have adopted the pattern, would not have felt abandoned or struggled as she did, and would have developed freer attitudes toward men; so that we are even forced to add that her love of her father and his early kindness to her were factors also necessary for the new pattern to evolve.

It may be lamented by some that we don't have an obvious scapegoat in cases like Irene's. We can't discharge our frustration simply by describing her father as cruel, since he wasn't, and certainly it wouldn't be fair to say that Irene deserved to suffer, having brought her own troubles on her head. To many it may be satisfying to believe that most injuries to the psyche are the result of wantonness on the part of parents. Not only does this view provide us with a scapegoat; there is advantage in thinking that our problems came largely as a result of intentional acts. If our parents harmed us intentionally, they must have foreseen that they were harming us, and this means that we ourselves may in the future influence people like them to treat children more benignly, and thereby avoid causing similar damage to future generations. One value of psychoanalysis was that it enabled us to feel like heroes as we suffered. We could regard ourselves, like children of some deposed king, as the victims of a conspiracy conducted by vile adults to destroy our hopes. On the other hand, to assume that harm has been done to us without intention on anyone's part would make us victims of calamity rather than tragedy, a much less glamorous position to be in, and, one which, most of us feel, is less pitiable. However, nature is more often indifferent than cruel. No one armed our parents with perfect knowledge of how to bring up productive and healthy children, and their mistakes have often been made without desire to harm us. Rather than slander them, our best approach is to learn as much as we can about how to foster healthy development, to cure ourselves, and to provide better contexts for future generations.

It is less important to define trauma precisely than to account for the significance of early experiences. However, if we do wish to preserve the concept of trauma, we must remember to think about traumatic constellations, to which the sufferer unwittingly contributes, rather than simply about painful experiences.

Will your divorce be traumatic for your child? It may be if you deal with him differently than in the past. If, out of fear that he feels abandoned by you, you sanction whatever he does, you'll probably make the divorce a worse handicap for him than it need be. Divorces too often leave both parents trying to show their love by relaxing their demands on their children, with the result that the child finds no rewards in behavior that he will need later on. It's never a favor to excuse a child from acting in ways that will make him feel productive and will generate his respect for other people. As an adult he may blame his parents for their failures and accuse them of not loving him; and his parents, by this time furious at his ill treatment of them and confusing their anger with lack of love, may even believe the charge. However, as I've suggested, lack of love is seldom the crime committed by parents who bring up their children and worry about their welfare; more often their crime has been that of exempting their children from having to develop behavior patterns necessary for their happiness later on. This is especially true of parents who get divorced.

Remember that love can be expressed by your taking your child's enterprises seriously, and taking seriously his disloyalties to you, as your child would almost certainly want you to do. Whether or not you now believe you were justified in getting divorced, the most helpful thing you can do is to resist the impulse to win your child's forgiveness by courting him inappropriately. And there's an interesting twist. So long as you beg your child's forgiveness, you'll never feel forgiven. As with other attitudes, we renew our guilt whenever we act on it, and thus by making demands of your child, you'll heighten your conviction that you have the right to make legitimate demands. By fighting against the total collapse of the standards you set for him, whatever your present belief about your divorce, you'll restore both your child's belief in you and your belief in yourself.

The desire *not* to be like a parent is surprisingly

often a factor affecting the development of personality. A thirteen-year-old boy, very close to his mother but considered unmanly by his father, had mixed feelings about whether to court his father by building muscles and trying to demonstrate courage or to accept his mother's interpretation that his father was really a brute and not to be admired. One day a stray dog ran across the yard and destroyed some flowers that had recently been planted. In horror, the boy watched his father tie the dog to a stake and kick him in the head; he avoided his father as much as he could after that. Minutes after the incident, the boy made the silent but firm resolution to modulate his tone and to be gentle with people for the rest of his life. The single experience was probably not determinative. The boy had doubtless already been groping toward the conclusion that his father was not to be emulated. Single experiences are rarely enough to account for drastic changes in attitudes or the adoption of new modes of behavior which cause such changes to endure. However, single experiences, when vivid, may cause evolving attitudes to crystallize; and when afterward the experiences are remembered, it may seem to the person that they alone accounted for the unmistakable change in the direction of his development.

Along with the change toward mildness in the boy's approach to the world, he developed, and began to intensify by a widening sweep of behavior, a morbid fear of acting in any way that seemed authoritarian. Among the problems he presented as an adult were that he couldn't control his children and allowed his employees to take merciless advantage of him. When I saw him he was a partner in an accounting firm and was unable to demand even of his secretary that work be done according to specifications and in time to meet deadlines. Fear of becoming like his father had been inhibiting him and making him fear his own aggression ever since his early teens. In the only sense that trauma is meaningful, the incident with the dog, and the events predisposing him to respond to it as he did, were traumatic for him.

In a case with an interesting similarity, a young man recounted vivid memories of a father who bragged about inventions and business prospects that never bore fruit. The boy's mother and older brothers considered the father an ass, though the father worked diligently as a waiter and devoted himself to making the family comfortable. The boy loved his father and became distraught when the family would talk disparagingly about him behind his back and when they smiled at each other on the front porch while he talked animatedly about his latest invention. The boy vowed never to make his father's mistake, and this meant never to make promises or to be caught in a moment of optimism which he believed would be regarded as foolish. He taught himself carefully to conceal his aspirations and even his glimmers of hope, and afterward continued to renew his conviction that any expression of enthusiasm was the height of foolishness. By the time he was fourteen he had made maturity seem to him synonymous with being controlled; and by the time he came to see me, he was afraid of revealing even his most modest aspirations.

There can be little doubt that traumas may occur at any age, since we always hold some attitudes hesitantly, renewing them by some of our behavior and undoing them by other behavior. Depending upon many factors, including our acuity and knowledge, we may intensify the impressions we draw from experiences, or allow them to wither rapidly. The would-be writer who has received adverse criticism may be tempted to give up writing, in which case he may conclude later on either that he was talentless or that the critics broke his spirit. On the other hand, if he forces himself to continue, he will almost certainly prevent the criticisms from becoming traumatic for him. I once held group therapy sessions for six professional writers, and one of the rules all of them found most helpful was to undertake a new project the moment previous work reached the hands of publishers. These writers all found that working protected them against forming exaggerated fears of the critics and of what they would say; by waiting for evaluation before continuing, the writers would have exalted the critics to monstrous importance.

We often allow our first love affairs to become traumatic for us. For instance, if after they fail, we elect to act more guardedly with new lovers or mates than we did with our first one, we are liable to prevent ourselves from ever again feeling as deeply as we did.

The sudden experience of having people depend on us is frequently traumatic. The choice to shirk responsibilities pushes us away from other people and predisposes us to make similar choices in the future. Such choices heighten our prejudices and make us feel less deserving of people's kindness. On the other hand, ministering to people's needs is the surest way of making us feel like members of the larger family of mankind, which itself as a result of our acts of devotion comes to seem benign. Acts of devotion are the best cure for cynicism.

CHAPTER 10

Paranoia

PARANOIA IS A prevalent illness in our society. In extreme cases it drives people to murder, and even in mild ones it holds them in states of agitation and suspicion and leads them, individually and collectively, to brutalize other people and to express prejudices of all sorts. We nearly all become paranoid once in a while. By certain of our choices we unwittingly make ourselves paranoid. Understanding the paranoid process can enable us to determine which these choices are and to avoid them.

The opposite of paranoid is "gullible." Paranoia is the morbid fear of being duped or abused; it is the disease we produce in ourselves when we overdo our efforts not to be duped or abused. Paranoia is most prevalent in people who have been taken advantage of repeatedly or belong to a group that has been discriminated against. It is a short step from taking warranted precautions to taking unwarranted ones, and the paranoid process consists essentially of overprotecting ourselves. We who have by necessity had to develop techniques of defending ourselves and who have made them habitual may find it hardest to relax those techniques at critical moments, when if we did so we would discover that the people we distrusted are more sympathetic than those who took advantage of us in the past.

Paranoia is also prevalent among people seldom exploited in actuality, whose fear of being taken advantage of has been generated by warnings—for instance, warnings from parents themselves unduly suspicious. As a result of expectations impressed upon them by parents, many women develop the propensity for paranoid actions with men. Among the women who tell us they've been repeatedly mistreated and abandoned, some have in actuality been treated well but have driven away one man after another by being accusatory.

The diagnosis of paranoia is, as a rule, applied only to cases in which the condition is extreme; in state mental hospitals it is made when there are delusions of grandeur or delusions of persecution. When either of these two symptoms becomes strong, it is nearly always accompanied by the other. If you think mistakenly that one person doesn't like you, you may be suffering from feelings of persecution. However, the belief that fifty people don't like you and are planning to force you out of your job contains more than feelings of persecution. It is grandiose, since it assumes that fifty people consider you worthy of their continued attention. The man in the street can hardly become paranoid without being grandiose.

On the other hand, from the premise that you are

invested with genius or divinity, and the observation that you are regarded as commonplace, it would seem to follow that other people are persecuting you. To be great without being celebrated is to be discriminated against.

Two other common symptoms are feelings of transparency and delusions of reference. The former are unwarranted concerns that people can draw conclusions about your motives and attitudes from comments you've made or from your involuntary gestures. The sufferer from severe paranoia sometimes believes he is so transparent that people can read his mind, read it from far away. To him there may seem no way of escaping his tormenters except perhaps by killing them, or at the very least by bringing them to the attention of authorities who will be able to restrain them.

Thoughts of reference are unrealistic presumptions that other people are talking about us—not necessarily with malice, just taking note of us. Two people at the other end of a bus are whispering. Are they whispering about you? If you're on your way to an extramarital affair and you think that possibly they know about it, it may seem plausible that they are. To play it safe, you turn away, and now you've unwittingly intensified your belief that they were referring to you in their conversation. Your own avoidant act has given you a sudden chill; and you get off the bus six blocks before your destination, just to be on the safe side. You hurry toward your destination, perhaps becoming distracted and not intensifying your feelings of reference further.

Even in mild cases of paranoia, we may see all the symptoms together; and since mild cases sometimes flare into acute disturbances, it would be helpful, I think, to use the word "paranoia" to describe conditions which though not severe are qualitatively identical to severe cases. If you characteristically think people don't like you, when in actuality they do or are indifferent to you, you are paranoid to the extent that your impressions are untrue. If whenever you've given a friend slight reason to be piqued, there seems to you a major chance that he'll want to end the relationship, you're probably suffering from a mild case of paranoia. Jealousy is a common variant of paranoia, and nearly all cases of jealousy are instances of paranoia.

Paranoid fears may be enlargements of warranted concerns, or utter creations, warp and woof. In the beginning and during the course of the illness, unless it reaches psychotic proportions, the sufferer from paranoia senses intermittently that the conclusions he is drawing about people are wrong. He may not voice his suspicions, knowing that if they're wrong he'll appear foolish, or fearing that if they're right and he expresses them, he will alert people to hide their attitudes more carefully. In the beginning he may be concerned that if he expresses distrust of people he will repel them; and he is well advised in this worry, since little displeases us more than having our kindness called into question by someone we thought was loyal. As he becomes surer of our malevolence, however, his concern about our adverse reaction diminishes, and he may even come to anticipate with pleasure our being aghast at his accusations.

Not all suspicious people are more prone to become paranoid than nonsuspicious ones. Whether we become paranoid or not depends largely on how we handle a certain kind of situation which we may encounter in any of diverse forms, and which we nearly all encounter occasionally. If, for whatever reason, we make the wrong choices in this situation, we produce paranoia and may intensify it, convincing ourselves that people are conspiring to harm us.

Once we've embarked on the paranoid path, decisions that will make us more paranoid come to seem increasingly reasonable, and those that would rid us of our paranoia seem to have less in their favor. The farther we move along this path, the more reasonable our paranoid acts appear.

It follows that the decisions which would save us from becoming paranoid require only slight courage in the beginning and become more difficult to make. By the time the disease is severe, the course of undoing the outlook must be plotted carefully, and takes some effort to pursue; and therefore a clear understanding of the *pre-paranoid situation* and how to handle it is the best defense against paranoia.

So significant is the handling of the pre-paranoid situation that even people who are relatively free of suspicions before entering it sometimes develop full-scale delusional systems once they are in it. I have nearly always been able to identify a pre-paranoid situation as the turning point in cases of paranoia that I have treated; however, most of my experience has been with nonhospitalized patients, and perhaps the generalization does not hold as regularly for the severely disturbed group.

The pre-paranoid situation is complete when two conditions are met:

1. We have made a strong emotional *investment* in succeeding at something—for instance, at being loved by our mate, or making good in a job, or being respected in the community.

2. We feel frightened about the possibility of being deprived of this precious satisfaction because of some *deficiency* in ourselves, which we either imagine exists or which really does exist. We may be concerned, for instance, about our sexual prowess; or we may feel inadequate because we are members of some minority group—e.g., Negroes, Jews, or homosexuals, and we have come to regard the personal characteristic we are concerned about as one for which we *should* be deprived of the success we seek.

The two conditions are closely related. When we've made a strong emotional investment, we tend to become subject to the second condition. The more heavily we depend on succeeding at something, the more unsympathetic we become toward our own shortcomings, real or imagined.

Once in the pre-paranoid situation, we ourselves answer a critical question by our actions. The question is, should I regard the person whose opinion is important to me as a friend or should I proceed cautiously with him, on the grounds that he might be unfriendly toward me if the full truth about me were known?

The willingness to gamble on other people's good faith and reasonableness protects us from paranoia. I'll elaborate upon this statement later on. Overcaution when in the pre-paranoid situation is the tactic that makes us paranoid. Our behavior later on determines how severely we suffer and for how long.

By defending ourselves against what we consider the outcome to be feared, we prevent ourselves from discovering what the other person's true attitudes toward us are, or would be if we exposed ourselves. Where the case is that our boss or lover or neighbor is really indifferent to the presence of the trait we are hiding or compensating for, we prevent ourselves from discovering that fact. Our overly defensive acts are, in effect, accusatory ones; they accuse other people of intolerance—accuse them in our minds even when those other people know nothing of our motives or our concerns about them.

Having begun to teach ourselves that there is strong

discrimination against us by the people whose acceptance we crave, we are apt to go on producing all the paranoid symptoms by acting in ways that seem to us only too reasonable. As we do, we may gradually replace our original concern about the deficiency with new and more complicated concerns. We imagine ourselves in other difficulties, so immediate and pressing that we may even lose interest in the relationship we originally held precious.

Whenever we invest an enterprise with great importance and reduce our emotional involvement elsewhere, we are unwittingly creating a pre-paranoid situation. Such situations need not be dangerous, but if you are prone to paranoia it is important that you identify them. A girl who fell in love with a young man from an old American family suddenly became ashamed that her parents were Italian. She concealed the fact from her boyfriend, fearing that if he learned of it he would find her unacceptable for marriage. Her parents lived in another state and she seldom mentioned them. Her own conscious avoidance of the topic of her family heightened her conviction that he would judge her adversely because they were not American-born. As time went by, she realized that if she now talked about her parents, he would recognize that she had withheld information about them and would dislike her for her subterfuge. Soon her fear of appearing duplicitous became as great as her concern over being Italian.

For several months, she centered her thoughts on

the young man. She stopped meeting girl friends for lunch and seldom talked to them on the phone. It was, in fact, customary in her social group for a girl, once she began a serious relationship, to dedicate herself to it, not relying on her other friendships for sustenance and paying minimum attention to them. Slowly she invested her romance with life-sustaining importance, and her feelings of inadequacy, bound up with her concern over being of Italian descent, tormented her. The torment reached its height when the young man proposed to her and she accepted.

Some weeks after that, when she was with her fiancé and a friend of his, the friend made a disparaging comment about Italians. Her fiancé said nothing. When the friend was gone, the girl made several snide statements about him, thinking that perhaps her fiancé would defend him and that she would finally verify her suspicion that her fiancé was bigoted. When again he said nothing, the girl suddenly got the idea that he and his friend had contrived the conversation to test her. They had wanted to see whether she would confess if given the chance. But how had they known? One of them must have spoken with Carol, her friend; and perhaps if Carol were angry with her, she would have told them.

The girl accused Carol of disloyalty and an argument ensued, during which Carol denied discussing her. Once in the conversation, Carol said that having been accused, she felt at liberty to reveal that the girl's parents were Italian. Actually, Carol did not do so, but as may be imagined, her threat helped spiral the girl's paranoid fears. The Italian issue did not arise again, but the girl, who was by now morbidly fearful of being exposed to ridicule, became so critical of her fiancé that she finally provoked him into breaking the engagement. When she came to me she realized that all her suspicions had been unwarranted.

Especially if you are prone toward paranoia, look out for accusatory tendencies and try not to contrive tests of people's good faith. Doing so will very likely intensify your suspicions, and at the very least, predispose you to think that such tests are necessary. We seldom find absolute proof that a suspect is innocent. Most evidence, even if it suggests innocence, can be interpreted in different ways; and by the very contriving of our tests, we predispose ourselves to feel that the worst is befalling us. The more elaborate the test, the harder it is for us to view it as having been unwarranted and the more likely we become to misinterpret whatever evidence we find.

The sufferer from paranoia encounters a particular kind of problem. After each of his tests—and he carries out a succession of them as he toys with his different hypotheses—he is in the position of having increased his suspicions by direct effect while gathering evidence suggesting that his suspicions are groundless. The problem, viewed from his vantage point, is this: he must reconcile the apparent benignity of other people with the fact that he feels more frightened of them than before. He does this by making his intuitive leaps, characteristically crediting people with more intelligence and concern over hiding their machinations from him than he has ever seen them display. Each new conclusion adds to his future expectations and, because direct effects account for much of the substance of our attitudes, the sufferer sometimes warps his own view rapidly and with little part played by others.

The process is especially vivid in people who pride themselves on their intelligence. A husband listens on the extension when his wife picks up the phone. She is talking to her hairdresser, and continues only long enough to set up an appointment. Her husband hangs up just after she does. By his own standards, his listening on the phone is not justifiable in a love relationship unless there is reason to be suspicious. By picking up the phone, concealing the click, and listening to the conversation, he has made himself more suspicious of her, even while gathering evidence that his suspicions are unwarranted. His eavesdropping, rather than anything he has heard, has increased his suspicion; and therefore the data do not account for his misgivings. However, to make sense out of his new perception, he feels he *must* make the data account for it. To do this, he makes his intuitive leaps. For instance, he speculates that his wife is arranging to receive her critical calls at her sister's home; and he even toys with the idea that the hairdresser's call was a signal—or that perhaps they had a code. He is proud of these inferences, and if he allows them to motivate new data-gathering tactics, he further intensifies his belief that there is complicity against him. He is sarcastic to his wife's sister, taking the license because she may be hostile to him, and this behavior intensifies that belief, as well as his original fear, no matter how she responds. By repeated experiment and conclusion he widens his suspicions and intensifies them. We can, in many cases, identify most of the individual ideas in the paranoid's delusional system as explanations he has devised to account for the outcomes of his experiments.

Nearly all the elements I've discussed appear in the following case. A young man told me that for a week and a half he lay in his room, shuddered when he heard footsteps outside, and felt convinced that his boss was coming to kill him. When his brother came across the country to get him, the young man, whom I'll call Peter, told his brother quietly that both their lives were in danger. His brother left, and returned the next day with a psychiatrist. Peter promised to commit himself to a mental hospital for treatment of his "agitation" upon condition that he could first visit his brother's children, whom he adored. His fears had extended to nearly everyone; it seemed to him that only his two nephews, ages six and nine, would not betray him, and he wanted to speak to them. When he saw them he wept.

The diagnosis of paranoia was made and he was released from a private hospital several days later in his brother's custody. He came to see me two days after that.

Peter's mother had been deaf from birth; she was

forty and his father fifty-nine when Peter was born. Peter's brother was fourteen years older and paid little attention to him. His parents were unexpressive; they provided for his physical needs but were indifferent to his emotional ones. When still very young, he came to believe it was senseless to turn to other people for sympathy. Though liked by his playmates he had no close friends; he dealt with his schoolmates as though they, like his parents, were indifferent to his personal struggles. He seldom discussed his personal goals or his concerns with people, on the assumption that no one would be interested in hearing them. Mainly by keeping all his communications impersonal, he reassigned to people he met the parts that his parents played, convincing himself that they were honest but unconcerned with whether they ever saw him again, would be tolerant perhaps but not sympathetic.

In adolescence he spent long hours by himself reading. He saw his schoolmates only in the classroom, never went to their parties. He was graduated with the highest honors from high school and won a full scholarship to the state university where he made journalism his major. In college he became widely known for getting good grades. Students came to him for help and some tried to become his friends; he was ready to answer questions and by his second year was tutoring people extensively. Always though, he treated them impersonally, not with the conscious aim of keeping his distance but because he had no idea of how to make intimate contacts with them.

Tutoring was the beginning of his social life. He liked explaining the subject matter of his different courses and enjoyed the avid interest that students showed when he talked. Students soon invited him to their gatherings, and before long he could count many of them as his friends. By the time he was twenty, there seemed to him no doubt that his being knowledgeable was necessary for his getting other people to like him, and he rapidly developed the ambition to become a great writer. During his last two years in college he worked hard at refining his writing style and he had five poems published in magazines by his last semester in college.

Meanwhile he dated a few girls but did not become emotionally attached to any of them. He didn't talk about his personal life and it never occurred to him to discuss the details of their lives with them. He was virtually invited by one girl to have sexual intercourse with her, which he did, and afterward he thought for a time that he was in love with her. For the first time he was able to discuss his career with someone. She considered him a genius and encouraged him further with his writing. When he graduated, he came to New York to work on a magazine during the day and to try to write a novel at night. He and the girl agreed that they would correspond, though each of them would go out on dates with other people.

Peter was friendly with two young couples who had left the state university and come to New York City when he did. He spent his first two weeks in New York at the home of one of them and then found an apartment. His first job was as an editor in a small publishing house. New York was lonely. The two young couples were his only friends. He visited them often, keeping their interest in him alive mainly by talking about magazines and books while they listened and asked questions. His girl wrote to him that she had become engaged to an instructor at the university, whose abilities she praised in the letter much as she had praised Peter's when she was with him.

Peter yearned for a woman like her, and wondered whether he should have asked her to marry him. In the few years previous he had surmised that people involve themselves emotionally, that they love and hate and quarrel and have reunions, that they enjoy sexual intercourse and go away together on vacations. He'd known nothing whatever of that sort of life, hadn't even known it existed, until recently, and now he very much wanted to find a place for himself in it.

The prospect of succeeding as a writer became more than a delicious fantasy. Success in a writing career now seemed to be the only way that he could possibly earn the money, the social status, and the recognition he needed to compensate for what he considered his lack of social skills. In his fantasies he was now placing the highest fulfillments that society offers to its most eminent writers at the feet of a woman, to show her that despite whatever impression she might have formed of him, he was worthy of her.

After four months his publishing house ran out of

money to pay him, and he was dismissed along with several other writers. He lived on his savings while filling out applications for other jobs, and then he was hired by a first-rate magazine. He was told over the phone to report at the beginning of the next month, which was ten days away. During those ten days he worried incessantly about how good a writer he was; and many times he fell prey to fears that he would not be able to write well enough to hold his new job. The fact that being a good writer was so important to him, that so many of his hopes depended for their fulfillment on his being able to write well enough to hold his new job, was in itself sufficient to heighten his concern over how much ability he had; and though he knew that he ought not construe his having been dismissed from his previous job as evidence that he'd done poorly, he couldn't help wondering during the ten days whether they had actually been disappointed with him or used the seniority explanation so as not to hurt his feelings.

He spent as much time as he could with his friends, who assured him that his vocabulary and writing style were better than those of most published writers, and he braced himself to report for work.

On the new job his boss gave him a week to study the files of the magazine. Sometimes the writing seemed better than he was capable of, and sometimes the very same articles seemed poorly written. At the end of the week, the boss gave him a writing assignment with instructions to complete it within three weeks. When they separated, he added that Peter should feel free to talk to him if he had writing problems to discuss.

That night Peter worried about whether he was proficient. One thing seemed certain. Mr. Adams would consider the first assignment a test of his adequacy. It annoyed Peter to think how heavily he depended on the judgment of a single person for his job security, but there seemed nothing he could do, and he resolved to work as hard as he could. For the first time it bothered him that he had exaggerated his experience on his résumé; he wondered whether he had led them to expect too much.

In a final desperate effort to cling to his job, he pressed himself to work every waking moment. He took his work home, and he stayed in the office during lunch hours. He shied away from conversations with his fellow writers, though he often watched to see whether they were as busy as he. When they were working and he was idle, he felt incompetent, and he busied himself. He rewrote passages that were perfectly all right, and unknowingly convinced himself by the rewriting that the originals had been inadequate. His fear that he might be deficient in writing skill led him to polish his work continually, and his doing so played a role in magnifying his fear. Note that we could not possibly understand how he made himself paranoid without appreciating the motivations for his actions as well as identifying the actions themselves.

So far, his exaggerated concerns centered almost exclusively on the issue of his own competence and whether he could hold his job; but soon he became preoccupied with the attitudes of Mr. Adams, who would decide in the end whether his writing was good enough. It seemed reasonable to play it safe with Mr. Adams, which meant to avoid him as much as possible, and when not possible, to treat him as though he might be unsympathetic. In the beginning, most of Peter's defensive maneuvers were unpremeditated and not conscious; however, he could recall many of them when talking to me.

Consider this one. It was lunch hour and he was the only one in the office where twelve people worked. He was eating a sandwich at his desk when Mr. Adams burst in unexpectedly. Seeing him, Peter made the rapid decision to push the sandwich over to the corner of his desk and to pretend that he was working. The motives for the act gave it its importance. Peter feared that his eating at his desk might seem irresponsible to Mr. Adams, or might even appear to him a show of contempt. Fearing that his first article would not prove up to par, Peter believed that he would be at the mercy of Mr. Adams when he handed it in. It was important not to leave wrong impressions now, since he would need an excellent reputation to offset the dissatisfaction that his article might cause Mr. Adams. Hiding the sandwich was in part an attempt to compensate for what he believed would be a failure in the future; it was an attempt to build his reputation with a boss who he thought would probably be unreasonable.

This seemingly insignificant act was one of many by which Peter increased his fear of Mr. Adams and by which he added to his belief that he really was a poor writer and that Mr. Adams would be unreasonable in judging his work.

Notice that if Peter had been worried about being Jewish, or Negro, or homosexual, or an epileptic, or Italian, and had hidden his sandwich believing that Mr. Adams might judge him adversely because of the particular trait he was compensating for, he would have added, ever so slightly, to his concern over having that trait.

Mr. Adams had apparently been looking for someone else, and seeing that the other writer had gone to lunch, he left as hurriedly as he had come in.

Peter wondered whether he'd been caught in his maneuver. He reconstructed the situation as well as he could, and then tried to go back to work.

He didn't take seriously his boss's offer of help. As a child he had developed the expectation that he would have to solve all his problems himself, or else leave them unsolved; and besides, by maneuvers like hiding his sandwich he had already heightened his fear and distrust of the boss. Thus both his early life and the more recent events in it motivated him to make the very choices which were worst for him.

By this time his fellow workers sensed that his temperament and interests were utterly different from theirs. They seldom spoke to him. Though they remained courteous to him, they stopped inviting him to join them for lunch. Peter now perceived his fellow workers, and not without some cause, as a homogeneous mass of young men and women, able to enjoy social interchanges and perhaps already having arrived at the unverbalized agreement that they would do well to avoid him. He envied their apparent friendship with Mr. Adams. When he handed in the article, Mr. Adams made numerous copy-editing changes in it; he was pleasant but Peter twice defended himself loudly when Mr. Adams shortened his sentences.

That night he spent many hours with his friends, one of the married couples, belittling Mr. Adams and speaking derisively of the copy-editing changes that Mr. Adams had made. The next day, when he found himself in an elevator with Mr. Adams, he could manage only a few routine comments, which he thought at the time sounded stiff. Afterward he wondered if Mr. Adams had detected his artificiality and could possibly interpret it. Meanwhile it became a topic of light humor in the office that he never smiled. First a girl mentioned it and then other people made reference to it. By then Peter allowed himself to talk to only one person in the office, a quiet family man named Vincent. When the two of them were in the office afterhours one evening, he asked Vincent numerous questions about Mr. Adams. Vincent answered them politely but succinctly. Peter blurted out that he didn't like Mr. Adams, and Vincent disagreed immediately, saying that Mr. Adams was a "decent boss." Peter became terrified over what he had revealed and begged Vincent not to repeat a word of it. Vincent promised not to. Peter got the impression that Vincent was looking at him strangely.

A few days later his worst fears seemed realized. He saw Vincent and Mr. Adams going out to lunch together, supposedly to discuss an article. Vincent helped Mr. Adams on with his coat. On the hunch that Vincent had betrayed him and that the two were planning to talk about him, Peter hurried with them into the elevator. He had left them at the restaurant, feeling uncomfortable at the last moment, when he realized that if they were going to talk about him, they would certainly not have begun while he was in their presence. In fact, it had seemed to him once or twice that Vincent had begun to say something and changed his mind. Peter's following the two of them to the restaurant had made it seem to him all the more plausible that they were in league and that his days on the job were numbered. At least they won't do anything violent to me, he thought; and then he wasn't so sure, since after all, Mr. Adams might consider him a serious enemy if Vincent revealed that he was telling people around the office that Mr. Adams was a bad editor.

Working on the next article was out of the question. First and most immediately, Peter needed peace of mind; and to secure it, he needed desperately to know whether Vincent and Mr. Adams were really talking about him. Perhaps his writing had been *good* enough to threaten them. He thought about them constantly, shifting from one pattern of speculation to another. He peered over his pages when in the office, and made occasional notes, but accomplished nothing.

A few days later, he happened to see a letter from his old magazine and addressed to his boss. It occurred to him instantly that Mr. Adams had written to his chief editor there. Now there was no choice but to stay late in the office and to read the letter on Mr. Adams's desk.

That night he went into Mr. Adams's private office at about eleven o'clock. Terrified, he made a mental note of how the letters were placed on the desk. He found the letter in question, opened it; and it turned out to be an ad. He put the letters back carefully in their previous places—an act which, as he saw it, was advisable, since it was barely possible that Mr. Adams had spread out the letters on his desk in a predetermined pattern before leaving. It frightened Peter to watch himself rearranging the letters on Mr. Adams's desk: he imagined Mr. Adams watching him. The thought crossed his mind that he might be insane. He pushed it away. Then he thought of himself as all alone in New York and wanted to cry. When he finished, he closed the door quickly and hurried into the elevator. He wondered whether he had replaced the letters properly, but got confused about their previous arrangement, gave up trying to remember it, and became more frightened. Once again, by defending himself against what seemed like a possible but unlikely occurrence (this time, it was the fear that Mr. Adams had been lying in wait for him), he made that occurrence seem more plausible, and now he credited Mr. Adams with a remarkable amount of intelligence and deviousness.

When the deadline came, he had only half finished his article. He was immobilized, unable to write a word, and it seemed obvious to him that now it was only a matter of time till he would be fired. He wondered whether the envelope had been used as a trick to see whether he would enter Mr. Adams's office, and returning to work without the completed article now seemed impossible. He was terrified of Mr. Adams and of everybody in the office.

On the following Monday he decided he would finish his article at home that day and return to work the next. He got up early and telephoned the office with an excuse. The secretary who spoke to him was polite, but she seemed to know that he was lying about being ill and even to have anticipated that he was going to call. Notice the concern with transparency, the feelings of reference and persecution, and even the grandiosity in this single conjecture.

After trying to write the article for a few minutes, he gave up in despair; he was convinced that Mr. Adams and the rest of the office crew were waiting to see the draft he would hand in, to find faults with it, and to ridicule him. Why not? He had given Mr.

Adams good reason to ridicule him, Peter thought. The next day he repeated the process and the secretary's voice on the phone terrified him. He stopped calling the office in the mornings and now he was certain that they were planning to fire him and were laughing at him.

He went out and bought enough canned food to last him a month, took his telephone off the hook and lay on his bed. He wished for a million dollars so that he would never have to work for anyone—wished with the fervor that only a truly oppressed person, or one suffering from paranoia, can wish for assurance of safety. There was peace when no one was near him. Sometimes when he heard footsteps outside he imagined that Mr. Adams was coming to kill him. He put a hammer under his pillow and touched it often with his fingertips to be sure it was there. However, he vowed that he would strike only in self-defense, and that if he were fired he would not take revenge. Though he thought they were coming to kill him, he would not report them. As he told me later, he would rather be hurt or killed than harm another human being. The fact that he behaved as he did during this tormented period certainly made his statement credible.

Two weeks later his brother came to town after being unable to reach him and learning that he had not been seen. Peter had not been answering his telephone. When Peter told his brother that the lives of the two of them might be in danger, his brother pretended to accept the premise, then left on a pretext and returned with the psychiatrist.

Peter's dependence on Mr. Adams was, of course, important. Very likely, a million dollars would have saved Peter his paranoid episode, though he might have become paranoid in different sorts of situations then. Also, note how Peter's imagined deficiency became increasingly troublesome to him as holding his job took on increased importance to him. In all likelihood, Peter underwent moments of paranoia earlier in his life; however, he would perhaps not have become delusional even this time but for his eagerness to hold his job and his worry about how capable a writer he was.

Though lucid moments become fewer as paranoia progresses, they sometimes punctuate even extremely paranoid interludes. Even the paranoid sufferer who commits extreme acts of violence may have occasional glimpses of reality—moments of doubt that what he is doing is necessary. It is largely because he is ready for action and unable to tolerate the suspense of not knowing for certain whether he is really in danger that he chooses to act rather than risk being harmed. By his very act of violence, he deludes himself further, intensifying his belief that the act was warranted, and so when we discover him after he has committed the act of violence, and he is more deluded than before it, our tendency is to underestimate the degree of option he felt immediately prior to acting. Crimes of passion, for instance, nearly always intensify suspicions, and have been considered in advance much more thoroughly than we are led to assume when we talk to the criminal after his act.

Freud believed that paranoia is always a manifestation of homosexuality, and in fact this belief became so widespread that the adage started in psychoanalytic circles: "Scratch a paranoid and you'll find a homosexual underneath." Freud also believed he observed that practicing homosexuals are less liable to become paranoid than "latent homosexuals," people who feel homosexual impulses but resist them. It's not hard to see what led Freud to his conclusion. The latent homosexual, more than the practicing one, is liable to feel guilty about his homosexuality and to view it as a defect for which he should be disqualified from relationships or scorned in the community. Being the one more likely to consider his homosexuality a disqualifying defect, he is the one more likely to fear that his impulses will be identified and to take the measures that make him paranoid. Freud's conclusions suggest that among the patients who went to see him and his fellow psychiatrists in Vienna, many if not all of those who became paranoid were responding to overconcern about having homosexual desires.

Overconcern about homosexuality is still a frequent starting place for behavior that produces paranoia, which is not surprising since discrimination against homosexuals is still widespread. It's a short step from hiding one's homosexuality to save a job or preserve one's respect in a community to hiding it unnecessarily from people who would be indifferent to it; and thus in many communities the homosexual is all but invited to act in ways that would make him paranoid. The practitioner who sees only the well-off financially would find that the paranoia among his clientele frequently sprang from fear of homosexuality. Among poorer people, those in the "out-group," other sources of self-loathing, being more rampant, would be responsible for a high percentage of cases of paranoia.

Nowadays, blacks in the United States are frequent victims of paranoia, a fact which should also be no surprise. The light-skinned black is more liable than the dark-skinned one to become paranoid because, his circumstance being less clear, he finds more temptation than the dark-skinned black to try to present himself as white. Devices like hair straighteners, which many blacks use on the premise that it is desirable to try to resemble whites as closely as possible, are instruments of paranoia. And of course one can only beg all blacks to shun the chemicals still widely sold as skin lighteners: blacks become their own worst enemies whenever they act on the premise that they are intrinsically inferior to whites and try to emulate them. Though whites have done blacks great harm in this country, they shall not again have as much power to damage blacks' morale as blacks themselves will have. If you don't believe that a personal trait is a deficiency, don't treat it as one.

Naturally, the strongest statement that can be made about how to avoid paranoia is—Try not to act on the possibility that other people will hold particular traits of yours against you and will be unsympathetic if they discover them. As long as your concern over what you consider a possible deficiency is mild, you'll almost certainly have the power to avoid unnecessary defensive maneuvers. Err, if you must err, in the direction of *revealing* the trait and being disqualified for it. If you've never incurred people's disfavor because of some personal trait of yours, you're either a recluse or are suffering from paranoia. An excellent rule is—Don't set up situations to see how people will behave in them, and don't ask people questions to test their honesty, loyalty, or any other personal quality of theirs. Even asking people to reassure you of their love, if you do so excessively, will undermine you. Your very asking them will increase your uncertainty, which will motivate further questions and will push you further toward paranoia. Once you've asked excessively, whatever answer you receive will be suspect. If the person gives you precisely the answer you want, you will feel it is ungenuine and that you've extorted it from him; if he says nothing, you'll be angry.

One indication that you may be becoming paranoid in a relationship is your feeling acute discomfort during silences with the other person. The constant need for reassurance generated by paranoia can make blank moments unbearable and can fill a day with suspenseful intervals. If you're at all paranoid, you'll probably find that most phone conversations with people important to you are unsatisfying or heighten your anxiety. Your devices to gain reassurance may be subtle, like telling someone you love him, to elicit a similar statement from him. Professions of love are often questions in disguise, and when this is so, they make us more anxious, whether or not we get the answer we want. Many people profess love and then accuse the other person of being cold, and the reason is they've made a request and haven't received an answer. If after expressing a warm feeling you feel needier than before, you've been using a ploy. Don't declare your passion for someone unless you feel it at the moment. You'll know your assertion is genuine if, after making it, you feel warmly disposed toward the person without his having to make a similar assertion. Mother and child seldom feel more anxious after expressing love for each other; "lovers" often do, and the reason is that the motives for their declarations are so frequently contaminated by fear of losing the other person.

The time to look out for paranoia is, as I've said, when success in a single relationship, or on a job as in Peter's case, takes on consuming importance. It's at such times that we're most apt to scrutinize ourselves and magnify our shortcomings; and of course, it's precisely at such times, when we feel we have most to lose, that we find it hardest to reveal what we believe to be our weaknesses. We're especially susceptible to producing paranoia when we work with other people in close quarters. If you work in an office where the same set of fellow workers interact with you daily, or if you're a student and must prove your ability over a time period to the same set of professors who are to judge whether you are competent to go into your chosen profession, your self-doubts and tendency to act in ways that will make you paranoid are likely to be high. Especially at such times, look out for the tendency to belittle other people, those temporarily out of favor, as a way to improve your standing. The fear that hostile or snide comments will be remembered is frequently the stimulus for concerns about whether other people are in league against you, and a starting place for paranoia. If you're not snide you won't have to worry about your listener's going to a cocktail party at which he'll meet the person you've disparaged. Any act which you think would, if it were discovered, jeopardize a relationship precious to you may tempt you toward paranoid behavior.

Because all-consuming investment is so often the predisposing condition for paranoia, it's advisable, if you feel you are in jeopardy, as a stop-gap measure, to diversify your interests and emotional attachments. The girl who has just become engaged would do well to honor her obligations to former friends and to keep them important to her. Preserving the importance of your commitments won't reduce your capacity to love the people most important to you, and diversification will give you the patience not to suffocate the relationship that you treasure.

Probably women are more prone to develop paranoia around their love relationships than men are, since women tend to rest their hopes on the success of their love relationships more than men do. On the other hand, because men depend more heavily than women on the success of their careers, men tend more than women to become paranoid in their work situations.

The readiness to regard as mentally ill overly defensive attitudes and the behavior that goes with them is different in different cultures. If one man in a neighborhood distrusts his wife and keeps her locked at home when he leaves, and if without evidence he regularly accuses her of plotting to make him a laughing stock by being unfaithful, his neighbors will almost surely regard him as paranoid, whether or not they use the word. However, if keeping one's wife under lock and key and accusing her of infidelity is common practice in a neighborhood, it is likely that no one in the neighborhood will consider such behavior unduly defensive. From our vantage point, we may, with justification, describe the whole society as paranoid regarding its women.

To take another example, if millions of people in a society fear foreign invasion and defend against it at great cost to themselves when no invasion is threatened, it is meaningful to describe the society as paranoid whether or not its members perceive themselves that way. Once again, though the citizens in question may not appear paranoid to each other, any more than natives who stick pins in effigies to ward off devils appear paranoid to each other, it is appropriate and serviceable to describe the society as paranoid. The main costs of paranoid acts are the same, whether these acts are seen as bizarre by one's neighbors or not. Overly defensive acts heighten agitation and suspicion, and often produce real enemies, sometimes fulfilling the expectations that motivated those acts.

CHAPTER 11

The Fourth Effect—Recognition

WHEN WE WANT to change our personality, our actions are the only keys available for us to play on. The principles given can help us determine how the keys we play will sound. The fourth is perhaps the most obvious. Our actions provide us with observations of ourselves; and in precisely the same way that other people judge us, we use these observations in constructing our picture of what we call reality. I'll use the term *recognition effect* to designate this fourth principle. Recognition effects are reached by a more intellectual process than the others.

The four principles—interaction, vantage point, direct, and recognition—are the only ones that I have been able to identify. It seems likely that other ways by which our actions affect our own psyches will be discovered. We have as many players in the game as care to play. People with no training in psychology and little formal education are as likely as anyone to give us important leads.

Here's an example of the recognition effect at work.

A twenty-three-year-old boy, being supported by his schoolteacher mother, called me to tell me that she was foolish. She had found marijuana behind the radiator in his room and, confusing marijuana with addictive drugs, screamed at him that he was depraved. Over the phone the boy rasped, "I can't stand living with someone so stupid," and I asked whether his reason for calling was to tell me this. "Don't you agree she's a moron?" he said, apparently not hearing me. I said, "She overestimates the potential dangers of marijuana," and he said, "It's unbearable to be around her." There was strain in his voice this time. My factual answer had not satisfied some need of his, a need I couldn't identify at the time. During a pause he seemed to be suffering. I said, "I'm going to hang up, Tommy; next time you see me, tell me why you think your mother's ignorance infuriates you." "All right," he said, sounding beaten, and I put down the phone.

At the time I couldn't answer my own question. I had asked it because of my belief in a general truth. When we seem to be angry about other people's limitations, the real reason for our anger is nearly always that these limitations either thwart us, make us feel foolish because we've relied on those people, or remind us of something about ourselves.

When I next saw the boy, we discovered his sore spot—the recognition that he was depending upon his mother for financial support. He was able-bodied and extremely bright; yet he'd lost the few jobs he'd taken. He had never in his life paid his own rent, and though he described this fact as unimportant, he couldn't help responding to it. His childhood dream had included being the head of a household and earning a living. He now disdained this dream. However, he had not destroyed it; and thus his life had come to seem like one long uncompleted task, and he was furious without knowing why.

The recognition that he was as capable of earning a living as his mother, and that he was unnecessarily depending on her, added to his misery. He had taken to searching out her mistakes and mocking her for them in attempting to find relief. But paradoxically, her mistakes made him feel worse, since if she could carry on in spite of limitations, so could he; her mistakes were constant reminders that he was avoiding a challenge not insuperable but reasonable. He knew as well as I did that if everyone chose the course of staying home and collecting other people's mistakes, no one would have steam heat.

I could understand the boy's rage because I had felt similarly during the years that I dropped out of college, believing I might never go back. I saw what I considered mistakes all around me, mistakes that I could describe with irony; but all the while I compared myself with people doing what I still wanted to do, which was to finish school and use whatever abilities I had. I tried to push such comparisons out of my mind, and sometimes belittled other people for diligence. But other people's performances constantly reminded me that I might be doing more. It's hard to avoid comparing what we have done with what we think we could have done.

Would it pain you to reflect on your own performances? One test is to ask yourself, Do I make extensive use of irony as a way of conveying ideas? If you do, you're probably very bright and not using your abilities.

Do you sit long hours with friends talking about the charlatans in high political posts, or making acrid jokes about legislation you don't approve of? Or about the insensitive gallery owners who are nowadays rewarding incompetent artists and not giving good ones like you a chance? What irony in your being excluded!

Irony is a device aimed at separating you from the throng and its criteria. If your need for such a separation has goaded you into adopting and developing an ironic world view, probably you are in doubt about being able to meet your own criteria. Irony may be the perfect instrument if one wishes to say things he might be beheaded for, or believes that his undisguised statements would be suppressed. However, be careful of irony: its aim may not be to hoodwink an authority but to hoodwink yourself.

Consider heavy reliance on irony as a possible cue that you feel angry and impotent. Rather than convert your anguish into irony, examine it; it may suggest the direction that your next efforts should take.

I've worked with a number of people who seemed always on the threshold of punching someone. By expressions of uncontrollable rage, some of these people had lost their jobs and cost themselves treasured relationships. In nearly every case, they were brighter than their accomplishments suggested, and bitter over not performing as well as they knew they could. Unhappy recognitions about themselves underlay their heavy reliance on irony. Others with no more ability than they kept them constantly aware that they were defaulting.

Rage is nearly always a response to frustration—and sometimes we cause the frustration ourselves. How would you feel if someone pursued you wherever you went and advised you against undertaking the things you most wanted to do? He told you not to go to college, you were too old; not to ask a girl for a date, she might reject you; not to indulge in a sexual practice, because it was immoral. You would perhaps want to assault him—or at the very least, to run away from him. Well, there is someone giving you such advice—namely *you*. And if he is as harshly critical as the person I described, it's understandable that you may be furious much of the time. The person who belittles you through your own lips is as much an enemy as a stranger who belittles you—and far more dangerous, since you can't simply walk away from him. If you too frequently say, "Well, I really don't know very much about the subject" or "I'm probably wrong but . . ." take the same attitude toward yourself that you would toward anyone else who made similar comments about you. If you do, you'll probably become enraged at first. But then, as you resist the impulse to belittle yourself, you'll almost surely like yourself better than you did.

Consider this recognition effect on the other side of the ledger. I overheard a man in a restaurant saying to his wife, "I don't care what they think; I know I did my job as well as I could for the thirteen years I was there." Interestingly, many people would consider this statement naive, which it cannot possibly be, since it contains no misconception but simply describes a reaction. Enjoying the fruits of one's labor is never naive; though in a society where such pleasures are not esteemed highly enough, empty people sometimes try to deprive us of them by belittling them.

We are taking recognition effects into account whenever we choose behavior with the knowledge that we shall be looking back on what we have done and judging ourselves by it.

Did you ever promise yourself not to patronize someone's store because he insulted you? In a week, you're faced with a decision. His store is three blocks closer than the one you would have to go to in order to keep your promise. Should you walk the extra three blocks, or relent? I consider this kind of decision very important, because of the recognition effects that must follow it. For your own sake, remember that a promise was made to someone mistreated back in the past, someone whose only solace was the hope the promise would be kept. That someone needs you now, and it's up to you to protect him or abandon him. Whatever you do, you cannot escape taking action toward that person, and if you damage him, *you* will suffer the consequences. It's not just the person back in the past who needs you; it's the person in the future; you, in the future, will need the knowledge that you kept your promises in the past.

By breaking promises made to ourselves, we weaken ourselves. If such promises are to be broken, the motivation must be that we think they were ill advised, not that we simply lost interest in them. Failing yourself through indifference is betrayal, and you will feel it as such. I assure you of this.

Recognition effects are among the severer costs of drug addiction. A young man suffers a war injury which causes him intense back pain and results in his being released from the service and sent to a veteran's hospital. There he is given morphine regularly for his pain. After being discharged from the hospital he continues to crave morphine, which he needs if he is to sit in a chair for an extended period without pain. The pain diminishes but his craving does not. His work record is spotty and he loses several jobs in succession. After six months of wandering and living exclusively on his disability pay, he discovers a way to buy heroin and tries it. When it relieves him, he becomes frightened and decides never to use it again. However, he breaks his vow and borrows money from his brother to buy more. He soon exhausts his credit with his brother, borrows money from friends on pretexts, and does not repay any of them. He is now lying regularly to the people closest to him; and, just as we are observing him, he is observing himself and loathing himself for his activities.

It's the beginning of a new month, and he makes careful note of the date and vows he will never use heroin again as long as he lives. He stops for a week and is proud, but goes back to it. He is afraid to go to a medical doctor, since the law demands that doctors report all addicts, and he dreads being put on a list. His friends now all know of his addiction; his anesthetized condition—the hills and valleys of his life—is obvious to them. But more important, *he* knows about his addiction and is condemned to reflect on his own behavior repeatedly.

By degrees, he destroys his credibility with himself. He does so not simply by taking the drug, but in consequence of his reflections upon his own behavior! Paradoxically, the addict becomes slightly healthier when he stops making vows he cannot keep—though, of course, his best hope would be to give up his addiction. The course of supplying all addicts with their wants until we can cure them, or forever if we cannot, has been suggested by many. Among its potential values are that it would immediately save the addict from perceptions of himself that destroy his hope and his belief that he is worth saving.

CHAPTER 12

Some Comparisons of the Effects

I'VE SAID that as long as we live, our character structure remains alive, drawing sustenance from the very actions to which it contributes. Our moment to moment choices nourish it, and if it appears to have congealed, that is only because it remains largely intact. In this chapter, I want to discuss the different principles in a little more detail. The more firmly we have them in mind, the faster we can summon them up when they're needed to explain our experiences, and the better we can use them to discover the choices that will produce the outcomes we want.

A mother believes her ten-year-old son isn't adept enough with money to buy his lunch at school; she insists that he take a sandwich with him each day, though the other boys his age are all buying their lunches. Money isn't the issue, since the school lunches are inexpensive. Let's look at the different effects that this single practice exerts on the mother herself.

Interaction effect. By depriving her son of his only regular chance to handle money, she interferes with his learning an important social skill. Later on, when they go to a store together and she sees him fumbling with money and confused about how to make a purchase, her observations play a role in reinforcing her earlier fears. They appear to provide her with evidence that she was right in her decision to make him take his lunch with him. The interaction cycle has been completed. Interaction effects always depend for their force on our influencing other people and on our being influenced by their response to us.

Most of us tend to be blind to the significance of interaction effects. For one thing, other people comprise much of the content of our thoughts; for another, our thoughts about people come to us in the guise of pure observations—like photographs barely affected by quirks of the camera. We look outside and think we are seeing what is there, whereas actually our own behavior plays a role in determining what we see. So strong is the illusion that our reactions to people are based wholly on our objective observations of them that when we change our attitudes toward people without seeing them, we tend to think we've made new discoveries about them as we remember them, not realizing that *our own behavior* since we were with them last may have accounted for the change in our view of them.

Think about the vantage-point effects on the mother who insists that her son take a sandwich to school with him each morning. She prevents herself from seeing that he may be able to buy his lunch as the other boys do. Unlike the interaction effect, this vantage-point effect does not depend for its occurrence on the boy's behaving in any particular way. If, as a matter of pride, he were to throw away his sandwich immediately after leaving the house each morning, deciding that it was worth his whole allowance to get on line with his friends and buy his lunch, he would be nipping the interaction effect described, but not the vantage-point effect. His mother, by suppressing evidence that she underestimated her son's ability, would predispose herself to go on perceiving him as incompetent as long as she continued insisting that he take his sandwich with him each morning.

Because vantage-point effects do not depend for their force on other people's reacting to us, or even on their observing our behavior, they occur much more frequently than interaction effects. We are seldom aware of them; and in the sense that they play a main role in dictating our reactions to other people, they are deeper than interaction effects. We know what we've done, and we cannot help interpreting other people's behavior in the light of what we have done.

Direct effects are the deepest, exerting their influence on all our perceptions. They are always unconscious, though once we decide to look for them, we can infer them and work with them. Every living human can verify that they exist. We produce them whenever we act. They are forever renewing attitudes and modifying attitudes; they are the main determinants of whether we incorporate new attitudes or reject them; their continuous flow causes our character structure to undergo constant modification at its edges and to increase in complexity. To compare direct effects with the others, suppose the boy had rheumatic fever when he was two and his mother, sedulously following a doctor's instructions, did her best to protect him from all stress at that time. Now he is out of danger, and the same doctor, whom the mother trusts, recommends that the boy be allowed to live a normal life. However, his mother decides to continue her precautions, just to be on the safe side. Protecting him from having to get on line in a crowded lunchroom is one of those precautions. In this case, all such precautions would play a part in renewing her long-standing belief that her son is still vulnerable to heart damage, no matter what the doctors say.

If the mother had recently heard that all public school lunchrooms were places of great jostling and stress, and allowed the possibility that this was so to enter as a motivation for insisting that her son take his lunch with him, she would intensify her belief that this was so. By continuing to act on that belief, she would hold it in place; and direct effects would account for the addition of a new concern in her life. Notice that if the exact same information about public school lunchrooms had come to her during a summer, when she had no opportunity to act on it, and if she forgot the comment before school resumed, she would not come to renew her belief in its truth.

Suppose that on a given day the mother seriously

considers letting her son buy his own lunch. The reality that he is old enough to do so has become undeniable. He is eleven. She looks at him and is frightened by the recognition that he is becoming an adult: his getting older means that she is getting older. Without thinking, she finishes making the sandwich and gives it to him. Now, for the first time, since fear of growing old has become a prominent motivation for her act, her performing the very same act increases her fear of getting older. By acting on a casual belief, she has heightened her concern about it, and by numerous other acts she may go on regenerating that concern and making it even stronger. If the fear had come at a different time and evaporated before she had so opportune an occasion to act on it, she would not have intensified it. As parents we have so many opportunities to act on fears about ourselves when we minister to our children that we run a high risk of intensifying whatever fears we had; many parents feel older while their children are developing social skills than they do later when their children leave home.

In contrast with direct effects, vantage-point effects operate chiefly as preservatives. Their most significant role is that of holding in place the beliefs renewed by direct effects. When the boy is eight and his mother's main motivation for giving him his sandwich is the belief that he is incapable of buying it himself, vantage-point effects prevent her from discovering that he is capable. Later on, when her main motivations have changed, the vantage-point effects of the same activity are that it prevents her from seeing that a woman may enjoy youthfulness, vitality, and a rich sexual life even if she has a son old enough to buy his own lunch each day. Whereas direct effects account for the variety and intensity of our attitudes, vantage-point effects furnish insulation against evidence that might, if we had it, lead us to discard these attitudes.

We can compare the three effects mentioned so far, in terms of what is needed for them to occur. For interaction effects to occur, other people must respond to us. For vantage-point effects, no one need respond to us, but nearly always where they are significant, we think we are eliciting some particular response: we are interpreting, or misinterpreting, other people's behavior, judging it in the light of what we have done. Direct effects occur even when no one responds to us and when we are certain that no one is witnessing our behavior. They occur whether or not the conscious motives for our decisions include thoughts about other people. Since all our acts are motivated, direct effects occur whenever we act. Through direct effects, the mother's every act in preparing the boy's sandwich, and even her planning what she will give him, may be playing a part in renewing her fear that she is getting old and her dread of old age. This would be so if concerns about getting old were motivations for her behavior.

When at some point she allows her son to buy his lunch in school, she is relieving herself of a chain of activities, all those that were involved in getting his sandwich ready for him. It follows that in stopping each of these activities, she is modifying her attitudes toward herself and her son. She may feel anxious the first day she lets her son go to school with money in his pocket instead of a sandwich in hand; her anxiety would be a consequence of her exposing herself to the recognition that a new era was starting. Allowing her son to use his social skills as he developed them would, however, gradually reduce her fear of the new era; she would find that life was at least as tolerable with her son taking responsibility as it had been while she was coddling him.

Recognition effects depend on direct effects, and this fact has important implications for us. For example, take guilt—our most celebrated emotion. Guilt (as distinguished from fear over being punished for a wrongdoing) is almost a pure recognition effect. To feel guilt, we must hold a set of ethics, believe in it with some conviction, and we must also believe we have acted in violation of those ethics. In other words, guilt depends for its existence on our recognizing some discrepancy between what we have done and what we think we ought to do.

Once we suffer guilt feelings, the chief determinant of whether we continue to suffer them is whether we allow our guilt to motivate new behavior. Atoning, for example, has this effect. By atoning we unburden ourselves at the moment. But because our motives for atoning include guilt, by atoning we keep our guilt alive. Acts of atonement may be unmistakably motivated by guilt feelings, or they may be acts which pass as kindnesses. It serves us to regard any act motivated by the desire to make amends for a previous act as atonement. We're atoning when after wronging someone, we do what we can to demonstrate to him and to ourselves that we won't repeat our transgression. A husband caught in an extramarital affair begs forgiveness. Years afterward, he still ruminates about his act and discusses it with his wife occasionally, apologizing for it. Still feeling shame, he shows special considerateness, making many sacrifices for her. Because this behavior feels righteous to him and relieves him of guilt momentarily, he doesn't appreciate that it is keeping his shame and guilt alive. Even where guilt has derived originally from a too brutal evaluation of ourselves or a misguided judgment, we may, if we are not careful, blow it up to monstrous size by our own choices of behavior.

In everyday life, we usually rid ourselves of guilt feelings in either of two ways. One is by stopping the behavior that made us feel guilty, and not atoning for it. The other is by undertaking new activities which revise our value system and eventually make the act that troubled us seem acceptable. Actions produce their own argument. However, it cannot be stressed too strongly that the latter route has dangers inherent in it. For in the process of erasing our guilt, we change our beliefs about what is right; and the replacement of our early ethics by new ones may be, in the end, more damaging to us than our guilt feelings would have been. In such cases, our problems stem not from the fact that our dubious actions continue to seem wrong, but that they come to seem right. The chief costs to us when we allow our early ethics to erode are the loss of all the unverbalized benefits that went with belief in them; these include the feeling that good *ought* to triumph, that people everywhere are important, and that integrity is a value we have a right to expect of others and ought to expect of ourselves.

Some people derive a sense of satisfaction from feeling guilty. From the recognition that they feel distressed over something they did, they conclude that they must be principled people at heart—in contrast with imagined culprits who commit acts as bad or worse, and feel no pangs of guilt afterward. Be especially wary of people who tell you they feel guilty over something they didn't do and couldn't possibly have done (for instance, over something their country did many years ago). They're very likely trying to shame you by getting you to contrast your seeming lack of humanity with their boundless humanity. Perhaps some of these people really do feel guilty; but I would guess that those truly troubled about their behavior are slow to make pronouncements about it. Guilt has positive value only when it relates to something we ought to have done and may get the chance to do in the future.

Also, be careful about lending money to people

who represent themselves as having great humanitarian instincts, who talk about distant causes and who act surprised when you reveal that you don't know anything about them. Many of these people feel they don't have to pay you back. Their rationale goes something like this: "How could someone as bountiful as I, someone who would readily give his life if mankind could benefit from it, default on a twenty-dollar payment to a friend?" Pronouncements of great concern for the world are among the worst sorts of data one can find in a potential creditor. I hope I'm not too late.

Like guilt, pride is mainly a recognition effect, stimulated by actions that seem to the person inconsistent with what he expects of himself. As we repeat acts that made us proud and carry out other acts like them, we make it impossible for ourselves to continue feeling proud of the same sorts of acts. As we lift our expectations of ourselves, the acts that made us proud come to seem less outstanding, and thus we absorb our accomplishments as well as our crimes, making them seem less conspicuous by repeating them.

CHAPTER 13

Fear and Anxiety

I WANT TO talk about two very important emotions —fear and anxiety. Physiologically, both involve the same internal changes, like increases in the rate of heartbeat and adrenalin production. To the sufferer the two conditions feel the same; both are unpleasant, ranging from discomforting to agonizing. Each is accompanied by a sense of danger, the difference being that with fear we can identify what we think is threatening us and with anxiety we cannot. One is afraid of going to war or losing his job, but one is simply anxious and doesn't know about what. There are borderline cases in which it's hard to know which word to use; the choice depends on how much knowledge we think is needed before one's condition can be called fear instead of anxiety. A girl is frightened of going to a party but doesn't know why; she is attractive and well spoken, yet spends most of her time alone. Does she stay home because of fear or anxiety? Fear, if you think that her identifying the party as the source of danger to her justifies using the word. Anxiety if you don't.

Since we need to know the source of a reaction in order to control it, the condition of fear is in a sense healthier than that of anxiety. Whether our aim is to relieve ourselves of the condition or simply to learn from it, our most useful first step is to convert our anxiety into fear, if we can. Anxiety is useless to us, makes us wretched and gives us no information. Fear nearly always suggests some course of action, and gives us the chance to extinguish the feeling if we are so inclined. It may be said that the chief argument against the extensive use of drugs and distractants is that they translate anxiety into euphoria, or into dullness; we don't hear the warnings of fear when we need them.

Once we've converted our anxiety into fear, we must examine the fear closely with several questions in mind. The first is, What person or group of people is frightening me? The second is, What information about myself have I gathered from knowing that I am afraid? Pursuing the second question often leads us to important information about values, attitudes, and beliefs which we held but were unaware of. Once we've answered these two questions, for us to extinguish our fear we must either remove ourselves from the stimulus, remove the stimulus, or alter our psyches in some way so that we don't remain vulnerable to the stimulus. I shall enlarge on this last statement, using examples, shortly. The temptation to discharge fear by expressing it as rage is one we must guard against. Assaulting other people when we're afraid takes us far from the sphere of our difficulty, leaves us as vulnerable as we were, and often results in behavior we regret later on.

I don't say it's ever pleasant to discover our failings. Many of our irrational fears are caused by shams we have been perpetrating, and it's never fun to discover that one has been a charlatan. However, if we painstakingly study an attitude important to us, and dauntlessly refuse to be driven away by disgust or shame, we can make ourselves feel heroic. We ought to cultivate the pleasure of feeling like heroes when we make inner explorations; it's especially welcome when we've just uncovered a fact about ourselves that we're ashamed of. We sometimes need such facts so badly that we're willing to pursue them, whether or not we suffer in the process, so why not take credit for courage if we think we've displayed it?

A few years ago, a married couple I knew mentioned someone I hadn't seen since I was twelve, a lawyer with whom the husband of the couple worked. Before I caught myself, I'd belittled him several times. Why? I asked myself. It made me anxious to think about Roger now, and yet I couldn't remember disliking him. The last time I saw him was when we'd played in the street. As I thought about it, the fact that I was anxious became increasingly clear. Then I realized I was afraid that Roger would come back into my life and do me harm. And the harm he would do would be to reveal that I wasn't really a marvelous baseball player when I was young.

I discovered then that I'd been imposing a hoax

about my former playing ability. I'd been a good player in college days, but not as good as I'd wanted to be, and I think the husband of the couple overestimated how good I was. I'd enjoyed his believing I was an exceptional player, and I'd made some quiet statements that helped his illusion about me survive. Together we'd watched a baseball game and I'd commented on the form of a third baseman in fielding the ball. My insight was good, and I think the technical knowledge it conveyed revitalized his opinion that I might have been a successful professional player if I'd wanted to be. The worst of it was that part of my motivation for the statement had been to suggest that very conclusion.

And thus I had given Roger, whom I hadn't seen in over twenty years, the power to discredit me by telling my friend that I wasn't an outstanding baseball player when I was young. Considering the matter again, I realized that my baseball-playing reputation still mattered a little to me, and I didn't want it to matter at all. I was tempted to tell my host that I really hadn't been as good a player as he seemed to think, and to admit that I'd exaggerated. By doing that, I thought, I could immediately divest Roger of his power over me and relieve myself of having to continue my subterfuge. However, confessing seemed awfully serious for the mood of the evening and unnecessary; and in the end, preserving my freedom from Roger would depend on my not pretending further that I'd been a better player than was the case, whether I now confessed or not. I decided to say nothing, knowing that if I dropped my fraudulent pose, neither Roger nor anyone else could harm me by describing my ability fairly and accurately.

Before the incident, I had no idea that my being esteemed as a baseball player was of any significance to me. Though perhaps the significance was slight, it apparently had been strong enough to goad me into belittling someone I hardly knew. How unreasonable we are sometimes in the things that matter to us! But of course we are the ones who make them matter.

Consider this next example in which I'd sustained my belief in a myth by more subtle behavior than bragging.

One day I was reading about the history of the guillotine and was surprised when I came to a list of important persons in France who had been put to death on the guillotine. The list included numerous well-known and accomplished people. Seeing the name of Antoine Lavoisier, the founder of modern chemistry, I suddenly felt anxious. At first I didn't connect my feeling with any particular name on the list. Once I did, I pursued the matter, pressing myself to discover why Lavoisier's name in particular had induced so much anxiety in me. Why had his death on the guillotine been more distressing to me than the deaths of the other people on the list? The answer came to me suddenly. Though I had pursued it, when I found it I felt as though it had all along been pursuing me and finally caught up with me. Apparently, I had believed that if I were kind and dedicated to science and to helping my fellow men, I could not possibly be put to death, especially by my own countrymen. I had nurtured the unexamined conviction that good contributions, and even good honest efforts, would protect me against being destroyed, no matter what else I did. When I saw Lavoisier's name on the list, I felt endangered and anxious.

Naturally, I knew that my expectation of magical protection was unrealistic. I knew that Hitler had put to death thousands of scientists. Early in life, my mother had given me to believe that somehow by working hard and acting honestly, I would protect myself against whimsical disaster. At least some part of my motive (only a small part, I like to think) for helping people and striving to be honest with them had all along been a secret desire to buy protection for myself. In extending myself to learn what I could and to make my best contributions, I had been renewing my own belief that as long as I did what I could for people, I would not be whimsically murdered. Without reflecting on the matter, I had apparently imagined I was buying inviolable protection for myself, and the killing of Lavoisier on the guillotine suddenly forced me to see that this wasn't so.

Each of us believes that he must satisfy some particular set of conditions as payment for the sense of well-being he wants. Our past actions, which resurrect particular attitudes, are largely responsible for the set of conditions that seems important for us to satisfy. There are those of us who think they must be intelligent, rich, guileful, and virile to deserve being esteemed by others and by themselves. To the person with this belief, the suggestion that he lacks any one of those qualities is a threat. Threats appear in many forms. I once saw someone sit in a crowded room and mutter curses at himself for minutes because he had made a mistake in guessing the capital of a South American country. Ten of us were playing a game calling for geographical information, and no one else cared about his own mistakes. However, this person, after muttering to himself, held up the game a full three minutes explaining to all of us why he had forgotten the name. Presumably, by his dedication to the pursuit of knowledge (and by other behavior which made knowledgeability a needed compensation), he had renewed his conviction that without his appeal as a knowledgeable fellow, all would be lost.

With such a premise, think how vulnerable he was to being undermined. Knowledgeable people often rest their sense of well-being on knowing facts, and thus they keep themselves more susceptible to becoming embarrassed at revealing ignorance than the rest of us are. If you have an avid interest, pursue it, but be careful about selling yourself as an expert. No matter how much you know, you'll make yourself tenser and more defensive around your subject than if you took no interest in it at all, and by the pressure you put on yourself you may contaminate much of the joy that the interest might have afforded you.

It serves us best, I think, to limit ourselves to the word "anxious" unless we know both the personal

tion to express our anxiety as rage. Above all, we must not condemn people merely because their behavior is not customary—a temptation very likely to arise in us when their behavior makes us anxious and our first impulse is to get them to stop. Remember that customs were instituted by people perhaps made anxious by the very kind of behavior now distressing us.

For instance, throughout the ages men have based their sense of well-being in part on the belief that as men, they are essentially smarter and more robust than women, lustier and better able to enjoy the fruits of sexual variety without harming themselves in the process. Many of our practices regenerate these beliefs in the minds of most women as well as men: the college boy's paying the check for the college girl, the boy's going to the girl's home to begin the evening, the boy's being the pursuer, his tendency to curb harsh language when girls are present. Such activities are, for the most part, dictated by custom. They need renew nothing but belief in the customs involved, and in the importance of observing customs. However, for millions, observance is also motivated by beliefs regarding intrinsic differences between men and women, some of which do not exist. The price of renewing erroneous beliefs, especially those regarding our own superiority, is continued vulnerability. Many men would be made anxious by a woman's saying to them, "Don't call for me on our first date; I'll call for you." And the source of their discomfort would not be simply the breach of custom but the feeling of being unmanned, since for them the custom has all along contained the erroneous idea that men are sturdier and that women need their protection. These men might belittle the woman for the suggestion, or even treat her shabbily; they would do better to examine themselves for the source of the discomfort aroused in them.

A good rule is, If someone's behavior seems repellent to you, think twice before you condemn him for it. The temptation to reach for the first available argument against the activity may be great. However, if you succumb to it, you will remain vulnerable to the threat imposed and unenlightened about yourself.

The best test of whether we've found the true stimuli for our anxiety and have properly identified the nature of the threat is whether the measures we take relieve us. If a sequence of stimuli, each one appearing as soon as we've removed the other, all make us uncomfortable or irascible, it's a safe guess that we're suffering from anxiety, and that we haven't yet identified the source of the threat.

The woman who puts too great a premium on appearing young may feel undone when a younger woman joins her group in a restaurant. Not knowing precisely how she is being threatened, she crouches slightly and talks in measured cadence, to heighten the contrast between her and the other girl, hoping to make the younger girl's verve look like immaturity. During the evening, the woman comments to the group that dresses of the sort the young girl is wear-

condition being threatened and the source of the threat. Not till we have converted our anxiety into fear and identified the nature of the threat may we make a practical decision about whether we consider it worthwhile for us to continue resting our happiness on fulfilling the condition. As long as we live, we must necessarily rest our sense of well-being on our fulfilling *some* set of conditions made important for us by previous behavior. We are victims of whatever value system we have erected and made important; and since this is so, and necessarily so, it is extremely helpful to us to exercise our options over our values consciously.

When I discovered that the personal value I held important as a condition for well-being had to do with my baseball-playing ability, it was an easy decision to act in ways that would allow the need to disappear. I was certainly not pleased over the importance I'd given to my having been a successful baseball player. You may not be pleased if after examining your condemnation of someone for a sexual practice, you discover that you've been condemning the person because of some irrational fear of your own. Congratulate yourself for uncovering the fear, and then try to determine how you've been renewing it. Stop the behavior and you'll be free of the fear and also the urge to condemn.

While searching for the behavior that is keeping some unwanted condition alive, don't be surprised if some, or all, of the activities that were critical bore no obvious connection to the attitude that they were holding in place. The pattern of experiences in your life has been unique, which means that the system of relationships between your actions and attitudes is unique. You are renewing myriad subtle connections. The test of whether the acts you've uncovered are sources of reinfection is trial and error, the only test in any scientific approach. Change the behavior and watch the attitude, not just the first day but after a few months, when you can eliminate from your decision any bias that might be caused by the jarring impact which we must always expect in the early stages when we change habitual behavior.

It would seem desirable not to hold important any condition for well-being which includes in its statement a comparison with other people. If you want to be humane, or strong, or rich, do your best to satisfy your ambition. However, when you make supremacy over particular people a condition for your well-being, you are dooming yourself to making your competitors important in your fantasy life. Most of us don't want to do this.

A dangerous situation arises when we can identify a person or group causing us anxiety, but don't recognize the condition for our well-being that is under attack. We recognize that someone is causing us pain but don't know how he is doing it. At this moment, it's hard to like him, and naturally the temptation to belittle him is great. When societies are threatened, they nearly always take action rather than examine the nature of the threat. We must not allow ourselves to do this. As individuals, we must resist the tempta-

imagined the girl's considering her strange, or possibly laughing at her, if she were to lose consciousness and the truth—that she was epileptic—came out.

I exhorted her to go, saying that even if she had an attack and the girl proved intolerant, the effect on her would be less harmful than if she stayed home and intensified her fear by allowing it to motivate her. As I told Marie, the other girl could, at worst, become only one person standing in opposition to her, whereas if she didn't go on the trip, she would increase her belief that people *everywhere* were intolerant of those who suffered from epilepsy.

My procedure as a therapist is, by the way, to encourage behavior only where it is understood that the patient will try it out, if he is interested, on a trial and error basis, and where its effects are easily reversible. Marie decided to go. Perhaps the desire to please me was one of her motives; however, even if this was so, I was convinced that genuine belief in herself was also a motive; and as I viewed it at the time, when she would eventually allow herself to develop attachments to other people, she would easily replace me by them. In any event, she did not suffer from excessive desire to please people, and both of us were happy when she left my office deciding that she would go.

That night she called me on the phone and reported that she had met the third girl, had disliked her and made the decision not to go. Then she suddenly became sad and attacked herself by saying that no one could possibly consider her acceptable for marriage, or even as a friend, if they knew she had epilepsy. Her outlook regarding her own epilepsy had changed during the five hours since I had seen her, a time period during which she had learned nothing new about epilepsy or people's attitudes toward it. How had that happened? She herself must have altered it by her decision to stay home that weekend. The effect of the choice—the enlargement of her belief that she was unworthy and would be considered so by anyone who knew she was epileptic—testified to its motivation, which must have been mainly that belief.

The reason she had given me for staying home was a rationalization, a fact which we could discover, since if dislike of the girl had really been her essential motive, the main effect of her decision would have been increased dislike of the girl rather than increased demoralization over being epileptic.

When I made my interpretation, Marie agreed hesitantly and then more firmly. She added that she had suspected her real motive all along. Before the incident, she had been building her confidence steadily for many months, and the decision had undermined her. One lesson she learned from it was that no matter how we rationalize our acts, we will experience the consequences of their real motivations; and, as she knew well, it would be worth fighting hard to resist acts that could intensify her defeatist view of herself.

ing are garish. If the girl defends herself and an argument ensues, the real source of the threat to the woman's comfort is camouflaged by the argument. If the girl were to listen patiently and thank the woman for her advice, the woman's sense of threat would probably become even more intense, there being no argument to obscure it. To reduce her anxiety, the woman snaps at a waiter and belittles her husband sitting across the table from her. At home she berates him again, this time for paying too much attention to the girl, and accuses him of flirting with her. If by attacking her husband, the woman again succeeds in diverting her own attention from the threat, she learns nothing. It would take a friend who saw that she always became irascible when younger women were present to point out the problem to her; and few people are willing to assume this role.

The classic case in which anxiety masquerades as a sequence of specific fears is that of the hypochondriac. Though he complains of new ailments each day, the underlying source of his discomfort usually has nothing to do with any of them. He would be better off trying to identify the personal conditions which he feels are being threatened than arguing with doctors that they have overlooked highly significant symptoms. Like the rest of us, the hypochondriac's best course is to try to translate his anxiety into fear and then to take whatever measures are necessary to remove the threats he uncovers.

CHAPTER 14

Backward Inference

THE PRINCIPLE of direct effect has a useful by-product—a technique that can help us identify motivations which we hadn't previously recognized. It is especially good for identifying paranoid acts, and has general use. Once we discover that a particular attitude, which we consider undesirable, has been entering as a motivation for our actions, and that we have been unwittingly increasing its strength, we can use the knowledge to stop ourselves from intensifying it further.

A patient of mine, a girl I'll call Marie, suffered occasionally from mild epileptic seizures. Nearly every weekend in the winter months she would go skiing with a girl friend who knew about the seizures and had helped her over them several times. Marie was hesitant about going away on one weekend when the girl had already invited another of her friends. She didn't want to be at close quarters with someone who didn't know of her attacks and who might think less of her if she suffered one during the weekend. She

afford to pay him did he derive pleasure from being charitable with those who could not. One must conquer fear in order to earn the opportunity to act with kindness, and to be able to enjoy the pleasures of being kind.

The technique of backward inference is especially useful in combatting what the psychologist C. A. Tripp calls "reversal effects." By a pattern of actions which we carry out identically over a time period, we may cause ourselves to feel first one way and then another. For instance, the very actions that at first sustain our liking for someone, and increase it, may, when circumstances change, become responsible for our disliking him. If at such times we stop the behavior temporarily and do not resume it until we recover our former attitude, we can avoid this effect.

A woman loves her husband and works hard to make her marriage successful. Not just love but a sense of duty, belief in the institution of marriage, and slight feelings of inadequacy are among her motives for eagerly sharing her life with him and working for their common comfort. After several bitter quarrels, however, she feels one evening that she has given him grounds to become disappointed with her and to leave her. So far, nothing is seriously amiss. Such feelings occasionally predominate in even the best of marriages. One secret of steadiness in a relationship is not succumbing to them, and this means not allowing them to motivate a new pattern of choices which would perpetuate them.

Consider the case in which this mistake is made. A young lady puts a cup of coffee at her husband's side while he sits sullenly in his big overstuffed chair, reading the newspaper. When, toward the end of the evening, he hints the desire for sexual intercourse, she is eager to engage in it. She has been hoping he will approach her, not because she has sexual desire but because she construes sexual intercourse as a way of recovering him. Naturally, with this motive, she enjoys the act much less than usual. One of the activities most significant in confirming their love for each other is now pushing them apart. By going to bed with him, she has intensified her fear of losing him, whereas if she had waited till sexual desire was once again her predominant motive, she would have enjoyed the act and it would have regenerated the same loving feelings for her husband that she had held in the past. We can only too easily damage our sexual desire for our mates by proceeding in sexual acts with them when our motivations are wrong for us.

The appearance of new motives can cause any habitual behavior to suddenly take on new meanings for us. We must learn not to push forward when we dislike the direction in which we are going, and to wait until attitudes arise in us that we are satisfied to renew. The technique of backward inference can help us do this. Knowledge we gain about previous motivations can give us critical insights when we're considering new activities.

By asking ourselves which attitudes we have enlarged, we can often discover motives for acts already completed. The discovery of an enlargement due to direct effect is the discovery of a motive, and often the motive is one we've overlooked or didn't want to see. Notice the tinge of paranoia that Marie produced by her default. One can hardly become paranoid if one repeatedly asks, How are my attitudes toward people changing, and by which actions may I be changing them?

The technique of backward inference can help us identify our own rationalizations in retrospect. If, for instance, we've told ourselves we did something out of kindness, when our real motive was either the feeling that we were undeserving or the fear of offending someone, we can use the technique of backward inference to discover the truth. If the main motive for our act had been kindness, the act would have intensified our warm feelings for our beneficiary. If, therefore, we now discover that we like him less than we did before doing the favor for him, and especially if we feel less psychologically secure after our act than before it, we may conclude, using the backward inference method, that we've made our choice not because of kindness but because of other motives.

I once treated a young internist who suffered from anxiety attacks. He had been in practice about a year and still felt trepidation whenever he sent bills to his patients. He told me that when they didn't pay the first bills he sent to them, he would invariably assume that they couldn't afford to pay him and he would not send them bills a second time. It was obvious as he spoke that he felt no warm glow about his dealings with these patients as he would if he were enjoying the fruits of having acted with kindness. There was tension in his voice when he spoke about sending out bills.

A few weeks later he told me that he felt cheated by his patients and angry with them when they didn't pay him immediately. Together we discovered that disbelief in his own ability was his main motive for not sending out fresh bills when his first bills were left unpaid. Not only did he resent the patients who failed to pay him, but he felt that these patients in particular knew he was a fraud and were blackmailing him. When on occasion one would suddenly appear in his office for treatment after disregarding his bills for months, he would minister to that patient with even greater concern than to the others. Afterward, he would suffer anxiety attacks. The magnification of his displeasure after dealings with these patients made his motives clear: the concern that he was incompetent and the fear of being discovered. If kindness had been his main motive, warm regard for his patients would have been magnified.

Sending bills to patients who hadn't paid him for months was difficult for him at first, but doing so was one of many practices that helped build up his confidence. Not until he convinced himself that he was able to make firm requests of patients who could

would call him a habitual smoker. Smoking would have particular meanings to him; for instance, he might consider it suave to smoke, in which case, upon stopping as an adult he would feel ungainly at first. Eventually, though, resisting the impulse would teach him, by direct and interaction effects, that he can appear as suave without a cigarette in his hand as with one.

Compulsions present a different sort of problem. The reason we can't cure ourselves of compulsions merely by resisting their urge is that their motive force derives from some underlying need which exists independent of the activity. The compulsive activity itself is aggravating the need, and in this sense is not merely a symptom of the need; but for the most part, other activities or life experiences are generating the need. The sufferer from a compulsion is choosing his activity as a palliative for his pain or discomfort. Deprive him of this palliative, or show him how to deprive himself of it, and he will almost immediately find others. Deprive him of all palliatives, and he will suffer as long as he remains goaded by the underlying need.

Activities that become compulsive are not always newly adopted ones. The activity may be an occasional practice of the past, like bridge playing, which suddenly takes on consuming importance because it becomes the most effective way that the psyche finds to reduce some intense craving. The habitual cigarette smoker who suddenly develops personal problems may, by using smoking to calm himself, convert the habit into a compulsion. Now when he tries to stop, he will become much more anxious than if he had tried earlier, and continued abstinence may not reduce his anxiety. He may find it impossible to subdue his urge without replacing smoking by some other activity and thereby reducing his underlying need. We may describe compulsive behavior as the attempt by the psyche of the sufferer to solve some underlying problem, one perhaps intensified by the activity (as is often obvious with the compulsive eater), but one that owes mainly to difficulties elsewhere in the psyche and seldom identified by the sufferer.

The attack on all behavior toward which we feel driven and which we consider harmful should consist of three steps. The first is to fight the impulse as though we were certain we were dealing with a habit. If we are in fact working against a habit, this first step will be our last one. The impulse will diminish and disappear, probably within a few months. If the first step fails, we may conclude we are dealing with a compulsion, a fact we could not have known before making our frontal attack and learning that it would not help. Our attempt to resist the impulse has served a purpose regardless of its outcome: it has either cured us or given us a diagnosis which we can rely on.

Our second step, if needed, must be to identify the underlying problem—the psychic contradiction making us anxious and producing the need which we have been trying to relieve with our compulsive behavior.

CHAPTER 15

Habits and Compulsions

THE FOLLOWING distinction proves extremely serviceable. A habit is a practice which we feel an inner urge to carry out but which urge, if we resisted it repeatedly, would diminish after a time and disappear. To say that playing golf is a habit, or that gesticulating when one talks is a habit, is to say that by resisting the inclination toward the activity, we could eventually break its grip on us. In contrast, we can't rid ourselves of a compulsion simply by resisting it. Though we can sometimes reduce compulsive urges this way, they return to torment us. Months, and sometimes years, after we think we've defeated our compulsion by resisting it, we feel it suddenly welling up in us again, and we must battle as desperately as before if we are to resist it. If we manage to subdue the impulse successfully this time, we are likely to suffer from severe anxiety or from other serious symptoms.

Perhaps the most dangerous of these is *replacement*. We discover that while resisting our impulse we have unwittingly allowed some other activity to assume increased motive force. By the time we make the discovery, we find it as difficult to resist carrying out the new activity as it was to resist the old one. We have subdued the enemy but he has given his power to a replacement. "I no longer verify many times a day that my door is locked; however, now I worry incessantly that the gas is escaping and will kill my husband and me, and I feel compelled to make sure the gas is off whenever I walk through the kitchen." "I'm no longer a compulsive horse-player but I find that if I don't smoke marijuana every day I'm depressed."

If we resist the impulse toward the replacement activity, we may be plagued with still other impulses and more anxiety. We encounter the urge for replacement activities when fighting habits too, but with compulsions they present by far the more serious difficulty. The problem of subduing the urge for replacements would be insuperable if we were to fight compulsions merely by using the head-on attack of resisting them, the method that succeeds with habits. Compulsions are different in their nature from habits, and they must be fought differently.

The fact that we can defeat a habit by resisting it means that the main urge for the habitual activity derives from previous practice of it. Teach an adolescent to smoke cigarettes and if he continues, the chief source of his urge to smoke as an adult will probably be the pattern of attitudes which survive mainly because he has been smoking. Where this is so, we

Having turned our attention away from the compulsive activity to the source of the anxiety itself, we now find that the problem is to resolve the anxiety, which means translating it into a specific fear and using whatever techniques we have at our disposal to rid ourselves of it. Perhaps some of the techniques mentioned in the section on anxiety will help; or, if the anxiety is of a paranoid form, those mentioned in the chapter on paranoia. The more we know, and the more consistently we are able to think of our actions as causal agents in our personality, the better able we are to rid ourselves of anxiety using whatever psychological principles we think will help us.

Finally, we must, after ministering to our need, partially or completely, try to fight the urge for the activity by resisting it, the very step we took before we were sure we were dealing with a compulsion. If we have greatly reduced the need which was motivating the activity, we shall find that we are now able to resist the impulse, even though we could not do so in the past. By our second step, we have converted our compulsion into a habit, and we can now defeat it by the attack that works with habits. However, be ready for difficulties even here. Some compulsive activities are also strongly habitual; that is, they derive a considerable part of their motive force from previous indulgence in the activity. Having converted the compulsive activity into a habitual one, we may still be faced with all the difficulties to be expected when trying to break a staunch habit.

Two characteristics apart from the strength of the impulse may make an activity difficult to stop. The first is insignificance. Habits difficult to identify may be surprisingly hard to break. When it is easy for us to smuggle our indulgences past the censor of consciousness, we have less control over an activity than when we can identify it easily. There are cigarette smokers, even inveterate ones, for whom it would be harder to stop a habit like gesticulating or biting a lip than to stop smoking. With smoking, lighting a match to a cigarette, which is a conscious act, provides a cue that can be used as a reminder; and certainly, buying a pack of cigarettes is an act that gives us time to reflect on whether we'll smoke. With gesticulating or biting a lip, we have no such reminders. However, we can devise reminders, and it is often helpful to do so. For instance, if we habitually engage in an act when angry, then rising anger can be a cue to be careful. Or with gesticulating, as one patient of mine learned to say to himself, "You're getting anxious; so watch out! Be careful, because you're about to wave your arms wildly and look ridiculous."

The second kind of habitual activity which is difficult to control is the kind that when carried out in moderation is serviceable or necessary. Indulgence per se is not the problem, but excessive indulgence. Overeating, which is usually compulsive but is sometimes habitual, is an example. Because the borderline between necessary eating and overeating is difficult to delineate, it's harder to identify violations of an eating plan than the alcoholic's violations, which are the very act of drinking an alcoholic beverage. Unlike the overeater, the alcoholic always knows when he is breaking his resolution, and this easy identification gives him an advantage in fighting his habit which the overeater does not have. If possible, the best plan when fighting a habit is to stop it altogether, even if we intend to engage in the activity in moderation later on. But, of course, when we need an activity for survival we cannot do this. Whenever we must distinguish between excessive and reasonable indulgence we face this special problem. Cleaning up your apartment is meritorious sometimes but when carried to excess becomes a disease. Subjective judgments are needed to establish the borderline, and they may be difficult to make.

Even seemingly insignificant habits sometimes put up trenchant resistance against being subdued. The moment we try to stop nearly any habit, we may be surprised to discover that the habit is more vigorous and guileful than we had imagined. Our impulse for it *increases;* and along with the impulse there may come a flood of thoughts which if we heeded them would convince us that our decision to stop the activity was ill advised. Included among these thoughts may be that this one occasion is different from the others we had in mind when we decided to stop the activity and that therefore on this one occasion we should disregard our decision.

In addition, when we resist our impulse, we nearly

always feel *incomplete* at first. The person who tries not to gesticulate may suddenly feel that his sweeps of the hand are eloquent and that what he is saying cannot be clearly conveyed without the use of his hands. If we disregard such irrational arguments, which we are best equipped to do if we have learned to expect them, we find that they diminish in strength. They often provide us with cues as to why we've adopted our habit in the first place.

A young history teacher who was a patient of mine agreed with me that her incessant criticizing of escorts was the main reason for their disliking her. For a time, she described her behavior as "expressing herself"; she would, at a moment's notice, put together an elaborate argument for women's rights and the fairness of saying what you think. However, it seemed to me that whether or not her points, taken individually, were sound, her behavior was out of control, and I told her so. When she disagreed with me, I suggested that she obtain further evidence by seeing if she could spend two weeks without criticizing anyone. She laughed and agreed to do so.

Within the first week she ran into trouble. While an escort was discussing France, he made a statement in passing which underestimated its population by five million. He had previously complained that she interrupted him too often and that she spoke stridently to him, and this time she vowed to let him finish his account without correcting him. At first, she felt thoroughly in command. It seemed to her that she could let his statement pass and still go on to enjoy the evening. However, as she sat across the dinner table from him, her impulse to speak became almost unbearable, and along with it there came to her the insistent message that he had deliberately underestimated the population of France in order to see whether she really knew her field. The key motivation behind her habit of criticizing, the desire to demonstrate that she was intelligent and could not be fooled by misstatements, suddenly became conscious and compelling as she listened to him. An instant later she blurted out that his facts were wrong; he said "Thanks" bitterly, and the conversation floundered.

Within minutes it became obvious to her that she had succumbed to the force of an irrational argument. Probably, her correcting people had been adopted as a practice to show that she was intelligent; at any rate, that motivation had entered somewhere along the line, and for years she had been renewing the belief that most misstatements were attempts to dupe her, renewing this belief by correcting them wherever she saw them. Restraining herself from correcting people would be a necessary step if she were ever to cure herself.

Irrational arguments in favor of an activity come to seem thoroughly reasonable to us when we fight a habit of long standing; they often give us information about why we began the habit, and they tell us why we're continuing it. If you want to know why you do something, restrain yourself the next time, and you'll probably find out.

When you resist nearly any habit of long standing, you are likely to feel a heightened impulse for the activity. There will be some anxiety—and also, rage, which we nearly always feel when we are deprived of something. Regard the flood of irrational arguments in favor of the habit as untrustworthy. You will be doing this automatically if you set a minimum time period for your attempt before you start. During the early stages you may feel incomplete. The activity continually restored a psychic balance, and now that you have stopped you may feel that a part of you is missing. Your habit satisfied a need, but the habit was also creating a need. You may feel unsatisfied and incomplete while the need is drying up.

Don't let any of the symptoms mentioned fool you into concluding that your habit is ingrained in a character structure which you can't change. The whole constellation of symptoms which we encounter when we try to break a habit merely illustrates the degree to which our mental processes are dictated by our emotional urges. With habits, we can diminish these urges by continued resistance, and when we do, the accompanying symptoms disappear.

I want to list briefly some hints which you may find helpful when fighting a habit.

1. Define the habit as precisely as you can. If it is *excessive* indulgence in some activity, specify what

you are going to consider the boundary line between warranted indulgence and excessive indulgence. This means that if you are an overeater and have failed in previous attempts at dieting, specify the upper limit of your allotment of calories, and count your calories as you go.

2. Designate a time interval for your siege on the activity.

3. During this interval, try to desist completely if this is feasible. If the problem is excessive indulgence in an activity which you need for survival, or which you must continue with, set your sights on not exceeding your allowable limit. Since most undesirable habits are not such extensions, the rule of stopping the practice completely can usually be followed. Once you've reduced your need for the activity by stopping it completely, you may indulge it in moderation later on. But don't make the decision to resume it till you've spent your designated number of months resisting it. For instance, if you're a habitual critic of other people, or a belittler of yourself, set your sights on stopping the activity altogether during the interval. Even if you think it's "being honest" to announce your shortcomings or to tell other people theirs, don't do it. Learn to view life from a new vantage point. Put yourself in the place of someone who is able to perceive the world as a non-critic, or as a non-belittler of himself perceives it. You'll find the vantage

point interesting. If you don't like it, you can always find ways of belittling yourself or other people later on.

If there is any doubt about whether you are the master of the activity or it is the master of you, your success at desisting completely will clear up the matter.

4. Look for cues as to when you're about to engage in the habit, and use them as reminders *not* to do so. Do you tend to engage in the habit when you are with particular people? Who are they? Particular *kinds* of people? Which kinds? Use their presence as a reminder to get ready for an increase in your impulse. Being forewarned, you will be the better able to resist it. And as I've said, your most dependable cues are your feelings. Do sudden feelings of incompetence motivate you to smoke? If so, you can attach a warning to these feelings. For the person concerned that he is drinking too much alcohol, rising anxiety may be an excellent reminder not to drink, or to take no more than one drink.

5. Don't judge the advisability of your resolution during your specified interval. Let's face it, enticements do go to our heads, which is why you've made your resolution in the first place. If your resolution to break some habit seems foolish to you now, and if you don't want to wait till the end of the specified period, at the very least make sure to carry out the

resolution just one more time. Reconsider it carefully when you're not subjected to the stress of the impulse. Very likely you'll realize then that you were the victim of an irrational thought pleading for continuation of the habit, and you'll be glad you resisted your urge. If not, you've given up nothing more than one opportunity for an indulgence.

6. Be wary of explanations of why you broke your resolution. It may seem to you that you drank because a close friend was present who you felt should not drink alone, or because you were going to a special interview and needed the drink for courage. Such explanations are dangerous. They becloud the fact that you broke a resolution—and that you did so through your own pure, free, unfettered will. The conclusion that your friend's need for a drinking partner forced you to drink implies that you may have to drink whenever you see him; the conclusion that you needed the drink for the interview implies that you will *always* need to drink before facing important people, or during tense moments of any kind. Justifications for breaking your resolutions pave the way to breaking them again. If you've just broken a resolution, you're better off with no explanation for your act and with whatever disgust you feel than with a handy explanation of why you broke it.

7. Create traumas and use them constructively. A bad experience caused by an unwanted habit can be a

good thing. If with the memory of the episode in mind—the embarrassment of being drunk in front of the boss—we stop the habit of drinking, we can use the experience constructively. By resisting our impulse each day, we can regenerate our embarrassment or disgust, which will in turn give us further motivation to resist the activity. If after the episode we had returned to drinking, we would have reduced the distress attached to the memory of the episode. As we sometimes sense, by our own behavior we can make a bad experience a trauma, and if we continue to resist the impulse we will preserve the value of the experience as a deterrent. A trauma is always a deterrent from some activity, and we can make use of this fact to help us break a habit.

Alcoholics sometimes say they drank excessively before an important occasion to degrade themselves so that they could use the memory as an incentive not to drink again. I seldom believe them. They drank for other reasons, their usual reasons—whatever these are. The retrospect analysis is a camouflage. I'm not saying, Create bad episodes to help you break a habit. Don't create them; stop now. However, if one has occurred, you may be able to convert the experience into a trauma and thereby use it constructively.

8. Expect that at moments you may feel more annoyed with yourself than you did before deciding to break the habit. In the past you paid little attention to the practice, perhaps assuming that it was more

under control than was the case. For a time, you now suffer the annoying experience of discovering minutes too late that you've engaged in the habit. This is the time your annoyance with yourself is likely to be at its height, when you can identify the activity unfailingly, but often instants too late to stop it. Take solace from the fact that your seeming helplessness isn't a sign of regression but of progress. You will soon be identifying the activity in time to do something about it, though constant vigilance will still be necessary for a period of weeks or months. When that stage is over, you will discover, to your pleasant surprise, that you have been free of the impulse while not even thinking about the activity. Whether the activity was a habit or a compulsion, you will find it easier to control than before, except that with a compulsion you will have lapsed into using some replacement activity to satisfy the underlying need, or else you'll continue to suffer from the need. By stopping the activity you have brought yourself closer to identifying the underlying need; and in many cases, stopping the compulsive activity makes the underlying need immediately apparent.

9. Remember that if you resist the impulse without benefit of drugs or medications, you will do more to defeat the impulse than if you don't. Hypnosis as a device to stop cigarette smoking has notoriously failed in experiments. The reason is, I think, that the person isn't making the choice to renounce the activity

but only the choice to respond to someone else's will. Renouncing a possible pleasure eventually diminishes our yearning for it, whereas being denied a possible pleasure does not. Agreed, your choice to pay a hypnotist a large fee may be a vote against smoking. So may your choice to submit to someone else's will. But your choice to submit is also an expression of disbelief in the power of your own will. In the end, your personal will is all that can save you and it needs your sponsorship. While under the effects of post-hypnotic suggestion, you are like the alcoholic snowbound in a shack, deprived of alcohol but not renouncing it; when the snow clears away, when the post-hypnotic suggestion wears off, your urge to drink may be as great as it was, or almost as great.

I haven't meant to rule out the occasional use of even the most artificial devices. For instance, where a practice is morbidly destructive, as a heroin addiction is, or as use of cocaine sometimes is, nearly any replacement for it may be desirable. If hypnosis can provide a successful replacement, the switch may be worthwhile. However, even here remember that the use of a gentle dose of an anesthetic helps more than the use of a massive one, for it leaves some part of the choice up to you. The best procedure when using synthetic devices is to gradually reduce their dosage as you develop the capacity to resist the impulse without them.

Any strong psychological need may underlie a compulsive activity, and any activity may be compulsive.

A little boy's urge to injure his father tempts him repeatedly to leave books in precarious balance on top of a bookshelf, where they may topple on his father's head. Dreading the possible consequences of his impulse, he spends many minutes pushing the books toward the back of the shelf before going to sleep at night. When his parents ask him to stop, he feels a hint of the desire to hurt his father. Lying in his bed in the dark, he feels deserving of punishment. He becomes anxious and calls for his father to come back and comfort him.

However, the comfort is of only temporary value. As long as the boy's unresolved conflict about his father exists, he must either suffer anxiety, continue to engage in his ritual, or replace it with another.

On nights when he is angriest with his father, his need to engage in the ritual with the books is the strongest. If while paying no attention to the compulsion, he comes to a new understanding of his father, resolves his conflict, and drains off most of his rage toward him, he will become relieved of much of his urge for the activity. The component of impulse remaining is that generated by the practice itself, which means that now his resisting the impulse will free him completely of it in the future.

If while the underlying rage toward his father was strong, the boy were prohibited from touching the books and no one went to his room to comfort him when he called, his anguished thoughts as he lay in his bed would perhaps include fantasies of killing his father. His being deprived of the compulsive activity would result in a surfacing of the urge. Not wanting to stifle our children's impulses, we tend to allow them compulsive palliatives, and thus when they do recover from compulsions on their own, it is usually by adopting new modes of behavior which reduce their underlying conflicts. Any solution to the frustration causing the boy's rage toward his father would reduce his need for the compulsive behavior.

Our understanding of compulsions teaches us something important: If your child seems driven toward some particular activity, consider the possibility that there is an underlying need unsatisfied. Is there a problem in his relationship with you? The compulsion may be a symptom of that problem. Children who are unduly given to rituals are children with unresolved problems.

Like all palliatives, compulsive activities tend to obscure from us the needs that caused us to use them, and lull us into underestimating the urgency of those needs. This is especially true when the behavior we make compulsive is socially acceptable. Such behavior needs no defense and therefore is not questioned. How many men play golf on weekends to hide from themselves dissatisfaction with their marriages? Ask any one of them why he plays and he'll probably answer that he loves the game. He may. However, the test of whether an activity is chosen or compulsively motivated is not whether we love it but what happens to us when we try to do without it. Golf, like nearly any activity, may become compulsive if we let it, even if it was no more than a fulfilling pastime to start with.

With nearly every compulsion there comes some reduction in the person's ability to enjoy the wide spectrum of experiences once pleasurable to him. When a craving becomes intense, it tends to become highly specific; other satisfactions will not do. Though friends and fellow workers may offer the same satisfactions to the sufferer from a compulsion, they may soon come to sense, correctly, that their value to him has decreased. Not just the compulsive activity but the multitude of preparations for it become responsible for the sufferer's inability to enjoy the rest of his life. To the compulsive gambler at the track, family members become people you have to talk to. Their desire to spend time with him becomes an annoyance; his children's excitement when he takes them to the zoo seems pale alongside his gambling experiences. Sufferers from severe compulsions, if they have been caught in the activity for years, will readily report that the activity—gambling or drinking, for instance—provides their only satisfaction.

When the indulgence occurs in cycles, as is necessarily the case with gambling and may be the case with any compulsion, the victim's life becomes cyclical. To the horse-player, the days shortly before a big race are the valleys he must pass through before reaching the foot of the next hill he is to climb, the next hill being the experience in store for him the day of the race. Compulsions furnish the illusion of forward motion—you are hungry and therefore you eat; you are in need of a drink and are taking one; you have an idea and are planning to bet money that it is right, the bet seems like a good business venture. It is only when he looks *backward* that the sufferer from a compulsion comes to fully appreciate its costs; in fact, one of his many reasons for continuing his compulsive activity is to save himself from having to acknowledge the amount of waste already produced by his indulgence.

The sufferer from nearly any compulsion of long standing, if he stops his activity before carefully resurrecting other sources of gratification, undergoes a "withdrawal reaction" like that which alcoholics report. It seems to him that his compulsion was saving him from the recognition that life is intrinsically meaningless. During this period of withdrawal there are few pleasures in his life, and the dominant feeling is numbness. It's up to him, during this time, to *produce* meaning, to identify attitudes that he wants to intensify and to find actions that will intensify them.

The problem of breaking compulsions is sometimes complicated by the victim's having evolved an elaborate philosophy which justifies his activity. A young man, meticulously dressed, told me quietly that he had been playing poker for high stakes four nights a week over the previous eight years, and that he usually lost. His wife had worked to help support them till shortly before giving birth to their first child. The young man, whom I'll call Edward, was still losing money in the games, and was unable to hold a job. His wife was now threatening to leave him, and though he pretended to be unconcerned about her, her threat had obviously been his motive for coming to see me.

Edward's father was the richest man in the neighborhood where the family still lives. He was generous with Edward, but hot-tempered and unpredictable. Partly in the effort not to resemble him, Edward simulated being calm when he was not, and later won admiration for being polished. As a teen-ager he was celebrated for knowing beautiful girls and for carrying large sums of money with him. In his neighborhood he was the first boy of his age to own a car. He would sit behind the wheel unruffled while driving it recklessly.

In my office he puffed a cigarette with the confidence of a defendant who believed there wasn't enough evidence to convict him. He didn't list among his problems that he had no way of earning a living. While arranging the handkerchief in his jacket, he told me calmly that he needed at least five hundred dollars a week to live comfortably. He spoke without a flicker of emotion. He was a study in detachment. One could see at a glance that appearances were his reality.

Edward said he felt a powerful urge to play poker whenever a game was scheduled, but he disagreed with his father's conjecture that his desire to play was compulsive. Perhaps because his father had lent him many thousands of dollars, which Edward had not yet repaid, his father was more willing than he to regard his poker-playing as neurotic. Edward described it rather as a desire to match wits with highly intelligent people, to enjoy their humor, and to learn from their insights. The other players all dressed well, as he did; and there was among them a mutual respect which he said he had seldom found among people too timid to gamble for high stakes. Edward once went so far as to tell me that it was courage that brought them together.

He told me that on certain nights after he had decided not to play, he found it unbearable to remain at home with his wife. He would nearly always break his vow. Toward eight thirty in the evening, when he knew the game would begin, whatever his wife said sounded tedious to him. He would wonder how he had come to promise that he would stay home with her. When he envisioned the other players seated around the green felt table, with cards and piles of chips in front of them, the very colors of the game excited him, and his urge to join the game would become unbearable. In the early days, he would provoke his wife into an argument and then storm out. However, that tactic became so obvious as to be silly. Later he would tell her that among the players at the game would be someone who could easily help him find a job—a story that worked for a while until

it too lost believability. His recent practice had been to assert without preamble that he was leaving. Being definite made it easier for him to go without feeling guilty.

Edward had expected me to request him to stop his gambling as a stipulation that I work with him. However, I knew he had tried to stop many times in the past and failed, and I was so sure there was a compulsive element in the activity that I decided to bypass this usual first step. Even without his stopping, we could discover many of his motivations for playing and proceed with therapy for a time. It soon became apparent that he was profoundly demoralized over disappointing his wife; he knew that her requests of him were reasonable. His standards for appearance were high, which made it hard for him to work at a job where his salary could be estimated and his worth per hour computed. He gave the impression at the poker table that he considered himself to be worth at least a thousand dollars a week, and revealing that he had taken a job for a hundred would puncture the image. However, he would eventually have to surrender this image and accept the fact that he was demoralized. This was the problem. If he could admit his demoralization, he would not need the refuge which his fellow poker-players provided.

To help sharpen his awareness of the problem, I made as my only stipulation for working with him that he get up early in the mornings. People who feel they're failing in life very often fall into the practice of staying up late at night mainly because mornings become unbearable. In the morning the fact that one has nowhere to go is undeniable, and it's hard to avoid comparing oneself with others eagerly rushing to jobs. The advantage of living at night is that one knows that most other people are also idle then; and thus at night it is much easier for many people to avoid feeling dissatisfaction with their lives. I wanted Edward to live through mornings simply to heighten his awareness of his dissatisfaction, so that we could talk about it. One of his first insights was that he would not want his son to respect a person like him, and that recognition saddened him.

It isn't pertinent to discuss my treatment of Edward at any length: the paths of cure are never the same for two people, though the principles which enable us to discover a path appropriate for us are the same for everyone. My main aim has been to illustrate how compulsions receive their nourishment from needs which the sufferer usually hasn't identified. Edward and I spent many hours discussing the attitudes of his fellow players and his attitudes toward them. We also discussed his feelings for his wife, and for his father, whom he realized he very much wanted to please. The fact that his father had been made brokenhearted by both Edward's gambling and his losing his jobs had suggested to Edward that perhaps he'd been losing intentionally to punish his father. The hasty conclusion that the consequences of an activity have necessarily been its intention has caused considerable confusion in recent years. People who draw this conclusion, having insufficient data to warrant it, sometimes try to justify it by ascribing unconscious motivations to the person who acted, motivations which make their claim about him seem warranted. Like Edward, some of us assault ourselves this way, forgetting that in doing so we are ascribing to ourselves perfect unconscious control over what our acts will accomplish. We ought to be more chary of ascribing unconscious motivations to people, especially since we seldom elevate them in the process. I've never heard of anyone's being credited with an unconscious good intention.

It is a frightening thing to feel that one cannot resist an impulse, worse when some compulsive activity of ours is harming other people. When someone suffers from a compulsion, rather than credit him with unconscious power and make him feel guiltier over what he is doing, we must help him uncover the needs underlying his compulsion and minister to them directly. And if we suffer from compulsions, we must do this for ourselves.

CHAPTER 16

Love Without Obstacles

Is it man's nature to be able to love only what he cannot fully possess? Some writers have said yes, that pure love, unquestioning and unfailing, depends for its sustenance on our finding our loved one imperfectly accessible to us, and is therefore impossible in marriage, where the mate is already possessed. Like many philosophical arguments, the issue is to a large extent psychological. When the philosopher finishes defining love (and, undoubtedly, to do so, he must accord to the term its spectrum of diverse meanings), we are left with the fact that some people seem to love their mates forever, unquestioningly, and that others find it impossible to love or respect those who become accessible.

The illness has no name, though it is widely recognized. Its victims are doomed to yearn for the woman who rejected them—as they yearn for the services of the practitioner who was too busy to see them, or the item they couldn't afford, while they underestimate the value of what they can afford. No matter how much they acquire, they feel unrewarded. Their experience is that whatever they most esteem and try hardest to attain declines in value from the moment they secure it.

Some of these people describe themselves as "loving the chase"; however, this is merely a retrospect attempt to account for their discovery that once they've made a relationship secure, it no longer satisfies them. As soon as such a person becomes assured that he is wanted and needed, the interaction shifts from courtship *by* him to courtship *of* him by the other person. The more the other person assures him of devotion, the faster he falls out of love.

Victims of the illness do not always propound the philosophy, described earlier, which would allow them to consider their condition universal. They are usually as vocal as the rest of us are, or more so, in declaring that inaccessibility ought not be a criterion of value in a love relationship or anywhere else. Like nearly all the rest of us, they assert that we ought to esteem people and things for their intrinsic value and not their market value. Intrinsic value does not increase with scarcity and decrease when the object is readily available. Market value reflects scarcity; and thus the problem I'm talking about is that of being unable to love and appreciate people and things for their intrinsic value.

Probably most of us have a slight dose of the illness I'm describing. By unexamined choices, we perpetuate the belief that easy availability decreases the value of what we own. The phenomenon is observable in everyday contacts, where our feelings are not as intense as in love relationships. The person afflicted with the attitude, if he is an acquaintance, thinks less of us as soon as he sees us unsure of ourselves, or weak and in need of his help. If he has known us for years and watched us learning our profession, or making the transition from childhood to adulthood, he may forever refuse to acknowledge that we have become capable. We are part of his sphere of familiarity; and in his thinking, no one from this sphere can possibly be as worthy as people outside of it. As an employer, he finds it hard to acknowledge when his underlings have, through experience, qualified themselves to handle better jobs in his organization. In some fields, it is common practice for workers to shift from one organization to another every few years, since employers refuse to give appropriate responsibilities and salaries to people who have developed their skills within the organization. The philosophy seems to be: If you're familiar and especially if you've needed me, then I cannot respect your skills.

As parents, we who suffer from this disease may refuse to concede our children's maturity, simply because we remember the days when they were helpless and dependent on us. It's a sad truth about many of us that our children would do better performing for someone else's parents.

How far does a prejudice against the familiar influence you? Do you regularly treat dinner guests better than the people who live with you? Are you regularly late for appointments made with intimates, and seldom late when you've made an appointment with a stranger? Do you fawn in front of professional men, and excuse them after they've kept you waiting for hours, and, in contrast, complain when someone you know keeps you waiting even a few minutes? If so, like millions, you are assuming, without considering the matter, that the time of people you don't know is more important than that of people you do, and your discriminatory treatment is renewing that assumption. There is nothing more precious than time, and yet perhaps the majority of us discriminate against the people closest to us when it comes to being considerate about time.

Perhaps the main cause of decline in feeling in love relationships is that after assuring ourselves we have secured our loved one's affection, we slack off in our efforts to treat them as respectfully as we did. While courting the person, we have kindled and intensified our regard for him, largely by our actions. Our affection has combined with our fear of losing the person to motivate diligent efforts to satisfy his expectations, as we interpret them, and to increase our value to him. Being unaware that our behavior has made a necessary contribution to our being in love, when we come to feel the relationship is secure, we see no reason to continue that behavior, and our love diminishes. When we don't replace our early courtship activities with new expressions of love and concern, we predictably cause our love, and even our respect, for the other person to diminish, and in many cases, to die completely. If we are to continue loving people, we had better go on courting them, even after feeling assured of their devotion.

A young man who had dissolved three marriages, each after becoming disappointed with his wife, came to see me at the urgent request of his latest girl friend. He didn't describe himself as incapable of sustaining love for a woman, but as unable to find a woman worthy of him. When we lose regard for others, our first impulse is to assume that they have deteriorated or that we have misjudged them, and thus sufferers from chronic disappointment are seldom aware that they have a personality problem. I saw the young man only once, since, having no problem, he decided there was no reason for him to undertake therapy. I remember his telling me that the one woman he had admired over a period of years was his boss's wife. He saw her only occasionally, at office gatherings and when she came to the office to go somewhere with her husband; but he always made a point of talking to her, and he frequently imagined that she would make him the perfect wife. Naturally, he thought so. For the sake of his job, he had made sure to treat her respectfully. And he always would, since he would never cherish the exultant moment of having her declare her need for him, and thus never embark on the pattern of behavior which would make her seem like every other woman who had disappointed him in the past.

There's a popular analysis of cases like these. The person who falls out of love is said to have a basically low opinion of himself, and to be able to respect only people who share that opinion of him. Upon discovering that someone he admires has high regard for him, he lowers his estimation of that person immediately. Supposedly, his reasoning goes this way: I am worth very little and therefore if you respect me, you must be worth little too.

Undoubtedly, some people do reason this way. However, the analysis is, I think, not serviceable in the vast majority of cases. One can always put together a convincing argument that someone has low self-esteem, and it's dangerous to rest an analysis on so vague a concept. Many psychologists have already spent too much time accounting for people's behavior in terms of attitudes they ascribe to the person but whose existence they have no way of verifying. It is hard to find even close agreement among psychologists on the level of someone's self-esteem. And even if I had made the interpretation that the young man suffered from low self-esteem, and he accepted it, how much would we have accomplished? It would still be incumbent upon us to discover those of his attitudes needing change and to identify the actions that would change them. Whether we suffer from low self-esteem or not, it is up to us to fight the lassitude that frequently befalls us when we no longer need to struggle for the affection of people we love.

There's an interesting pattern in many of the marriage "switches" we read about. Mr. and Mrs. A have come to loathe one another, and are barely on speaking terms. The same is true of Mr. and Mrs. B. However, Mr. A has always primped, worn his best suit, and been gracious and attentive in the presence of Mrs. B. Mrs. B has reciprocated in her way, and more than once has openly contrasted Mr. A's behavior with her husband's.

Mr. B and Mrs. A have also been debonair in each other's presence, and a similar relationship has started between them. What appear as two love relationships form and are sustained over the years, and eventually, after some episode, the switch of marriage partners seems natural. However, the participants soon slacken their good treatment of their new marriage partners, when it seems no longer needed; and as was predictable, the two second marriages suffer the fate of the earlier ones for exactly the same reason. If former husbands and wives are brought into each other's company by children, they may renew their courtship of each other, and regenerate love that seemed to be gone entirely.

Some of the most disrespectful people I've ever met have married shrews, after considering many potential partners seriously. Their friends marvel at their eventual choice. The reason for it is that only a person who demanded good treatment mercilessly could have deterred these people from generating disrespect. Among the men I'm talking about, some seemed relatively happy. Though bullied, at least they'd found someone they could go on respecting.

The belief that others will esteem us in proportion to our inaccessibility motivates a variety of tactics—all bad, since either they fail immediately, or they succeed but have harmful repercussions. Instilling jealousy in people is one such tactic. What the other person does while jealous may, as you expect, intensify his desire for you. However, if his motivation for courting you isn't affection but fear of losing you, when you put aside your tactic, it's predictable that his attentions will come to a halt. Because fear was at the heart of his trying to win you back, you can expect resentment once you have gone back. We don't like people who send us into the lion's cage to get the glove they dropped there. Since making people jealous is, in the end, little more than instilling fear in them, we may expect the advantages of the tactic to be short-lived. All techniques designed to create spurious inaccessibility for the sake of heightening our apparent value are undesirable for exactly the same reasons. In addition, whenever we consciously use a tactic in a relationship, we renew our belief that the tactic is needed to keep the relationship alive; and thus the use of tactics, whatever they are, robs us of intimacy with people.

The problem of loving only what is inaccessible occurs frequently in men with strong sexual inhibitions. Psychoanalysts have used the term "split-imago problem" to describe one form it may take. The man with this problem has developed the feeling early in life that there are essentially two kinds of women in the world: those who, like his mother, are to be treated with reverence, and in no other way; and those who, being fallen women in his view, are undeserving of his respect. Members of the second group he considers fair game for seduction but ineligible for marriage. He may regard sexual advances that he makes as tests of whether a woman is truly a madonna, a member of the first group. To preserve her lofty status, she must resist him. Where the problem is acute, the man may find himself unable to become aroused in attempts at sexual intercourse with the woman he has married. However he has perceived her earlier, his marrying her has made her a madonna; and perceiving sexual intercourse as an assault on decency, he feels that the act is inappropriate with his wife.

To the sufferer from the split-imago delusion, all women fall rapidly into one category or the other. It is important for him to make his distinctions quickly, since his whole method of operation varies depending on which kind of woman he thinks he is dealing with. In the presence of the madonna, he must refrain from using off-color language, watch his manners, and apologize if he acts improperly. He need do none of these things with the other kind of woman. I have seldom met a man whose attitudes showed no trace of the split-imago delusion and its attendant prejudices. Women are often right in believing that if their boyfriend seduces them, he will lose respect for them. They would do well to identify symptoms of the split-imago problem in men, since the attitude will cause them difficulties, whether they become classified as madonnas or as fallen women.

Among frequent manifestations of the split-imago problem are the man's derision of women who have been, in his view, promiscuous; his use of words like nymphomaniac, which suggest the dehumanizing of women; derision of people whose sexual behavior is not sanctioned by society, especially derision of homosexuals; his demand that you appear like a madonna, for instance, that you dress more formally than particular women on whom he thinks sexier clothing is appropriate. To split-imago sufferers, madonnas are expected to come from loving families with clean personal histories, which means that preoccupation with your family history may suggest an attempt to classify you. An almost infallible sign is a man's assumption that society's stereotypes all apply to you. You are expected to be passive, to resist his sexual advances, to be revolted at perversion, and to yearn for marriage and children. Remember that even if you are all of these things, it is up to him to learn the facts from you, rather than superimpose his expectations on you. When you're with a split-imago man, try as you may, it may be impossible for you to convey to him your innermost feelings, your fears, and your yearnings. His perception of you has already been formed—a perception which, since you are unique, can never be wholly accurate. As perhaps has been implied, if you are well able to identify your underlying attitudes toward life and are willing to express them, you will be best defended against becoming involved with a man who may someday consider you descended from a madonna to a whore.

CHAPTER 17

Inconsistency: Real or Imagined?

AN OLD MAN came to see me six months after his wife died. He told me that he'd been thinking about her incessantly. He still seemed bewildered by her death. After accepting condolences from their many friends, he'd withdrawn from people completely; he'd gone to work in his liquor store each day and then went home, not visiting either of his two married daughters and not talking to anyone except his customers and assistants in the store. He asked me what there was to live for; and with no answer ready for him, I said, "We'll find out."

I asked him which activities he had once enjoyed. His range of interests was narrow: his home, his wife, his children and their problems, an occasional dinner out and a vacation once a year. He looked at me as though my questions were pointless. I continued asking them in rapid succession, doing my best to appear to him purposeful and well satisfied with the answers I got. So far I was bluffing; but I knew that he depended upon my bluff, having considered carefully whether to go to a therapist at the urgent request of his daughter and deciding to try it as a last resort. I was happy when after our first session his daughter told me on the phone that he was willing to return. She scheduled the time of his next appointment for him.

Nearly all of us will at some time be confronted with the problem of having to motivate an aged person after the death of someone he loves. However, consistent with our disinterest in the aged, few of us have been willing to pause long enough to take the problem seriously. When one of our parents dies and the other is left with inadequate psychological resources to enjoy his life, we're apt to consider the difficulties of the remaining parent an irksome occurrence rather than evidence of a deep psychological problem which ought to command our full attention. Does our disinterest reflect mere lassitude? Is it that older people don't carry our names forth into the next generation and that therefore we don't take the trouble to cultivate their respect? If so, our painstaking work with our children is suspect in its motivation. More than we'd like to believe, we devote ourselves to helping the people who we think will be in a position to help us later on, and thus even many psychotherapists don't consider older people worthy of their professional time. Among the many effects of our prejudice against the aged is that the predicted outcomes for personality change in older people are often much worse than they ought to be, and because of pessimistic prognoses, older people are often discouraged from trying to change themselves. When I taught in college, I found that older people who had returned to take courses after many years were unmistakably better students as a group than the younger people. Many of my colleagues told me they'd reached the same conclusion, and one can list reasons why older people are often better therapy risks than younger ones. Chief among them is that older people are better able to postpone gratifications and readier to acknowledge the inescapable contract: that one must perform in order to achieve. Whereas the usual problem with children is getting them to take other people seriously, with adults it is getting them to take themselves seriously. Older people are perhaps as guilty of the prejudice against the aged as younger people are. This was the case with the man I've been talking about.

For many years, he said, he and his wife had been friendly with several couples about their own age. After his wife's death, these friends had telephoned him urging him to come over for dinner, and one friend had invited him to be a weekend guest. He had glumly refused all these invitations, and now their calls were becoming more occasional. Why should he see them? he asked me. Whether or not they mentioned his wife on the phone, they always made him think of her, and after hanging up he would feel worse than if they hadn't called. His daughters and their husbands always mentioned her, which was why he didn't want to see them. He'd visited each of his daughters exactly once since his wife had died. On each trip the mention of his wife had made him morose and he'd been glad to get into his car and leave.

He said that he'd sometimes enjoyed reading detective stories but hadn't read one since his wife died, and he wouldn't take a vacation because he'd planned to take one with her and now she wasn't alive to go with him. I asked him whether he had enjoyed playing with his grandchildren on his last trip, and he said, "Not really." But I caught a faint smile on his lips when he said so. I couldn't interpret it, and stayed on the subject. I asked him whether he had enjoyed playing with them while his wife was alive. "Very much," he said. "My wife and I always brought them presents and we couldn't wait to see them."

"How come you don't enjoy them anymore?" I asked, and he said he didn't know. "I guess I can't enjoy anything."

"Did you bring them presents when you went out there this time?" I asked. He said, no, and I asked him why not. "That was something my wife did," he said, and he described her as wonderfully kind. He drifted into telling me anecdotes, one after another, leaving no doubt that she was charitable and conscientious. He apparently felt best when talking about her, and I encouraged him to go on. He became animated while extolling her virtues.

At the end of the hour, he said, "Look, I don't

think you can help me. I like talking to you but I don't think you can help me." As he spoke I got the impression that there was more behind his wanting to avoid me than despair. No longer gloomy, he was agitated now. He was angry with me.

I told him in no uncertain terms that I thought he ought to come back at least once more before deciding whether to stop completely. When he was gone, it occurred to me that perhaps I'd had no ethical right to ask him to return. How far do a therapist's privileges extend? Does he have the right, no matter how much he thinks he knows, to make the suggestion that a patient solicit his services? Or is it his ethical obligation as therapist to remain no more than an implement helping patients accomplish only personality changes that they express desire for? Difference of opinion on the answer to this question frequently leads to conflict between patient and therapist, and I think that anyone considering going into therapy ought to think about the question explicitly and answer it for himself.

As I thought about the old man, I realized that if our roles were reversed I would have wanted him to exhort me to come back. However, I realized too that I could not in good faith continue for long charging him money and demanding his return. My answering service told me the next day that he himself had called to schedule an hour with me.

When next I saw him, he said he felt quite a bit better. However, as far as I could see, he was as morose as he had been, and his life had remained essentially unchanged. Perhaps he was telling me the truth, but perhaps he was using the statement as a ruse, complimenting me as a way of escaping from some interpretation which he feared I was readying but which I myself could not identify. He said that the nights were by far his worst time because he was alone with his thoughts. I suggested that he call me late that night if he felt acutely depressed, and he looked at me as though I were insane. He talked about his wife some more, and then blurted out that he would keep seeing me if that was all right.

During the next few sessions I worked at understanding his feelings and at identifying the motives for his behavior patterns. How could he make his life happier? It would help if close friends didn't mention his wife, he said. However, when I asked him whether he'd asked any of them not to mention her for a while, he became livid with rage. "I would never do that," he said, and for an instant I thought he might storm out of my office. He changed the subject, but I brought him back to it later on. "Do I understand you to say that you would rather not see your daughters at all than ask them to forgo talking about their mother for a time, until you feel able to discuss her without suffering intense pain?" This time, tears came to his eyes, and after a minute he muttered that such a request would be pointless, since the sight of their house was enough to make him despondent. 'Surely you must have at least one set of friends," I said, "who don't make you despondent, and who would gladly heed such a request." "I couldn't ask anyone not to talk about Martha," he sobbed, and again I pressed for a reason. But again he changed the subject and I decided to let it go, making a mental note to return to it. He was praising his wife again at length, and I listened.

During the next few sessions, I occasionally searched through his friendships for someone who would, if asked, indisputably honor my patient's need not to talk about his wife. If he was to find respite anywhere, it would be with such a person. He mentioned a Dr. Philips and his wife, whom he had known for thirty-seven years, and who had besieged him with invitations for dinner after his wife had died. I broached the question immediately. "Suppose your friend Ruth died," I asked, "and Dr. Philips begged of you not to mention her for a while, how would you feel about his request?" "Oh, I'd understand in a minute," he answered.

"Then would you please explain to me why you don't take them up on their offer to visit them, and make the same request?" I asked.

He repeated, "Don't ask me to do that," and I answered, "I'm not asking you to do anything, but we must discover the reason you won't do it. That reason may be important."

Again he answered, "I wouldn't do that." And then he became furious and said, "I don't even *want* to have a good time up there." For a moment the two of us were silent, thinking about his last statement. Not having planned the statement, he had conveyed in it more of his underlying thought than he'd intended to convey. Behind his refusals to consider my suggestion was the powerful belief that enjoyment of his life after his wife was dead would be an outrage against her memory. His smile at acknowledging that he had enjoyed playing with his grandchildren since his wife had died had been a smile of guilt. It was as though he'd betrayed her even in that moment of enjoyment. Loyalty seemed to demand of him that he minimize all differences between him living and her dead.

He was again telling an anecdote about his wife's generosity, restoring her to life in the telling, and feeling exhilarated. Pleasure in talking about her was not a violation of his taboo, since to him when he spoke about her, it was as if she were there.

During the weeks that followed, I brought to his awareness his guiding principle that it would be wrong for him to enjoy experiences now that his wife could no longer share them with him. He had, at the time of his wife's death, allowed that principle to motivate numerous choices, decisions not to experience pleasure. Afterward, the circle of avoidances had widened, and over the months the entire pattern of his eremitic life had reconfirmed his belief that fruitful living would dislodge her memory. By the time I saw him, he had converted this belief into a firmly held conviction.

While he was talking about his grandchildren one day, I asked him whether he thought it would be betraying his wife to find pleasure in playing with them. He laughed. I was chipping away at his logic, not with any hope of helping him by logic alone but to open up the possibility of new behavior, which might give him a different vantage point. As far as personality change is concerned, logic is worthless without action. My therapy plan, as I sketched it then, was to show him where he was deliberately forgoing pleasures on the premise that grasping for them would be disloyal—pleasures which, by his own testimony, his wife would have wanted him to enjoy. Recovery would be up to him; he would have to introduce gratifications into his life, and that was what he did. Doing so allowed him to perceive that there was no inherent contradiction between cherishing his wife and continuing to enjoy his existence.

The death of his wife had been a trauma. It had plunged him into despair and claimed him as an unwitting accomplice in darkening his outlook. It took more than a year for him to convince himself (by choosing new behavior and regularly reviewing his attitudes toward his wife to make sure they had not changed) that his seeking satisfactions would not lessen the value to him of the woman he had loved and lived with for almost fifty years.

A wide array of personality problems, many of them seemingly very different from one another, stem from misguided beliefs that two attitudes or practices are incompatible. Wherever the culture teaches us spurious distinctions, or that two attitudes are irreconcilable, our tendency is to act on what we've learned. By our behavior thereafter, we renew our belief that these distinctions are real. Where the distinctions involve other people, we become guilty of prejudice, and where they involve us directly we pay the price ourselves—that of sacrificing productiveness and pleasure, unnecessarily.

Freud's concept of the libido is relevant here. The libido, according to Freud, is a quantity of psychic force which exists in different amounts in each of us, and which generates activities. We pour our libido into being artists, or into building bridges or writing books, for example. Though the amount of libido in an individual is not measurable, the assumption is that his quantity of it does not change, from which it follows that as we spend our libido, we deplete our supply of it. What is important about the theory for our purposes is that it reflects an attitude which many of us hold but don't examine. The belief that there was a fixed quantity of psychic stuff in him was implicit in the old man's thinking that if he used that stuff in acts of enjoyment, he would deplete the amount available for cherishing his wife. It was not simply that enjoying himself seemed disloyal: he feared that doing so would deprive him of passion.

Freud wrote that the inhibited person is pouring much of his libido into the fight against his own impulses. A major purpose of psychoanalysis, as he formulated the process, was to "free" quantities of libido so that the patient could use his supply to fulfill himself. From the theory it followed that when we invest libido in new people, we reduce our capacity for investment in old ones. Young men who were unable to form love attachments were sometimes described as committing so much of their libido to their mothers that they were unable to love anyone else.

The psychoanalyst Erich Fromm took issue with one of the conclusions that Freud's libido theory demanded. Freud had described the narcissist as unable to love other people because he uses his libido in loving himself. Fromm observed that unless a person loves himself, he cannot love other people. But how are we to arrive at loving ourselves? Each of us must discover the activities that intensify whatever self-respect he has. We must learn to act in ways that produce love of ourselves, and love of other people if that is what we want to feel. If we are to preserve the libido concept, it must be appreciated that all our actions, however they affect us at the time, are also heightening our commitment in some direction. Even the decision to avoid someone is, in this sense, an investment—an investment in the belief that we ought not see him again, for whatever reasons we decided not to see him this time. If the person has repeatedly disappointed us, by ending the relationship we've increased our desire to know people of the kind we thought we were dealing with. It follows that the only way of increasing our supply of libido is by acting. There is nothing so wearisome to us as inaction, and nothing so stimulating as making decisions. This fact is important to know if you're a parent. Your greatest possible gift to your child is the opportunity to act responsibly. Children with psychological problems need this opportunity even more than others.

I was treating a divorced woman who was extremely worried about her son. There was no man in the home and he was copying her too closely for her comfort. At nine, he was the only boy on the street unable to throw a ball. He kept to himself; he was laughed at by other boys, and he threw up his arms in front of his face whenever there was a loud noise. His mother, who was poor, had registered the boy at the neighborhood mental hygiene clinic for children, but he was months away from being seen by a therapist.

I had at the time been working for about a year with a thirteen-year-old boy, well developed for his age. His father had recently deserted the family and the boy yearned for him. The boy was a sports enthusiast. Sports gave him his only regular contact with men: they talked to him directly from the television screen, telling him the scores of the games, and giving their opinions of the players and predictions about the future. The boy was himself an excellent athlete.

It occurred to me that Tommy might do well to teach little Leslie how to throw a ball, and that Leslie could profit greatly from the relationship. Tommy's allowance was a dollar a week, hardly enough for him to go to a professional baseball game. With pay of fifty cents an hour for teaching Leslie how to throw a ball, he could go more often. There would be many benefits for Leslie. He would have a boy to imitate, and I could teach Tommy a few tricks about the sorts of things to teach him. Tommy could improve his capacity for kindness and his facility for making close contact with people different from him. There seemed nothing to lose. New experiences may pain us but they seldom harm us unless we develop modes that perpetuate unfortunate attitudes.

Everyone agreed to the plan except Tommy's mother. She complained that Tommy spent little time with his younger brother as it was, and that if he became the tutor of another boy, he would spend none. I urged her permission for a trial period, and she consented. The boys took to each other immediately. Among the benefits of the therapy was that Tommy, through his teaching, *increased* his interest in how his brother threw a ball. He enjoyed his new vantage point; and without my saying a word, he spent more time with his younger brother and expressed more interest in him than he ever had in the past. His mother's fear that he would deplete some store of stuff proved unwarranted. From what I could gather, Leslie profited from the exchange. Tommy certainly did.

Don't worry about using up your store of libido—of

capacity for commitment. Two activities that seem psychologically incompatible to you may not seem so after you've tried them both for a time. You may have psychic energy for both.

CHAPTER 18

Rehearsal

THERE CAN BE immense advantage in rehearsing precisely what we want to say if a given situation arises. If we've been snide or have allowed some comment to pass without expressing how we felt about it, and if afterward we regret our handling of the incident, there ought to be no embarrassment about asking ourselves what we would like to have said, and what we would say if the exact same situation were to arise again. In retrospect, we can sometimes identify where our difficulties stemmed from; and just as it would profit countries to look at history and develop policies which would guide them when in the heat of fire, it is often extremely helpful to discover how we've contributed to misunderstandings that could have been avoided if we'd expressed ourselves precisely and to the point. Of course, we wouldn't want to rehearse our every comment to someone. However, our experiences enrich us only to the extent that we learn from them, and the discovery of what we wish we'd said is sometimes all that we can salvage after a blunder. The right phrase will convey our message, help us avoid sarcasm, satisfy us that we've taken care of ourselves, and give us our best chance of holding our relationship on an amicable course if we encounter a difficulty like the one we studied.

Even so, there are people who object to thinking in advance about any statement they are going to make. Mainly they argue that rehearsal would kill their spontaneity, or would make them inflexible and easy prey for the other person, who has not been burdened by having rehearsed and who is therefore flexible to respond at the moment, which the rehearsed person is not. Some object to rehearsing on the grounds that planning any statement is taking unfair advantage of the person to whom it is to be made. They perceive rehearsing in any form as guileful. To most of these people, rehearsing is acceptable when the plan is to burst into a boss's office and demand a raise, but becomes wholly unacceptable when the other person is a loved one.

It is perhaps true that rehearsed performances often sound stiff. However, the main reason is that in most situations for which we've seen the need to rehearse, we're in conflict about whether we have the right to say what we've rehearsed. The stiffness we feel is a reaction to fear; and remember that feelings of artificiality are an almost invariable reaction when we undertake a new mode of behavior. As we become accustomed to expressing ourselves in the ways we've rehearsed, the need for rehearsal diminishes and disappears and so does the stiffness. Even if this were not so, rehearsals would have significant value for most of us. There are at least some times in our lives when it feels urgent that we make a statement which is fair and complete. When we feel we're being misunderstood by a loved one, for example, the cost of sounding stiff seems trivial alongside the advantage of making sure we've been clear. Unless we know we've presented our own impressions accurately, it may be impossible for us to interpret the other person's treatment of us.

The conclusion that rehearsing is cold seems to me wholly unwarranted. We ought never describe any act as warm or cold without taking into account its motivation. The substitution of slyness for passion is cold, but rehearsing need not be this. There is nothing cold about trying to understand why you're having difficulty in a love relationship. And if you dislike yourself for past performances, there ought to be no taboo against deciding in advance what you will do if a situation like some previous one arises. If strong impulses to do the thing you think is harmful beset you in such situations, it's likely that one reason you succumb to them is that you haven't yet identified a mode of operation of which you would be proud. By rehearsing you can fortify yourself. There are people for whom careful rehearsal is necessary if they are ever to change styles of behavior and shift underlying attitudes.

Especially when trying to alter a behavior pattern of long standing, we are likely to find rehearsing new behavior helpful. Why not arm ourselves with as much awareness as we can when combatting a set of impulses firmly established by previous behavior? If the spirit behind the technique is right, planning our behavior in advance can sometimes enable us to build bridges to people who might otherwise not have been accessible.

A woman in her fifties complained of great difficulty in preserving a relationship with her son. Though each loved the other, they found themselves arguing all the time. The son was married with children of his own, and his mother, who was wealthy, would buy his family expensive gifts. The son was torn between taking the gifts (he was somewhat exploitive) and rejecting them to prove that he was grown up. He resented his mother for forcing the gifts on him, but he also, I think, disliked himself for depending upon her. His mother was annoyed with herself for trying to win him with purchases; and during a session with me, she decided that for the sake of both of them, she would follow the plan of not offering anything for a time.

The son continued trying to get what he could, using devices like telling her what went wrong in the house and what had to be repaired. The mother sensed correctly that he was asking for help; but more important from her point of view, she could hardly resist the impulse to offer it. Sometimes she blurted out offers and at other times bluntly asked him not to discuss his difficulties with her. In each case she disliked herself afterward; her offers left her feeling abused, and she saw that being blunt was pushing him away. The only path to preserve their relationship was for her to allow her son the freedom to say what he wanted to say, without her volunteering anything, except in a real emergency.

I asked her what such an emergency might be, and she mentioned the need for medical help, the need for his children's tuition at school, and several other needs. She decided that for a six-month period she would volunteer nothing unless one of those needs arose, and when she spoke she sounded satisfied. She reviewed the list of them in her mind and then wrote them down. She decided that if her son mentioned other needs, she would under no condition offer to help him; if some unexpected difficulty arose in his life, she would not change her plan on the spot but would go home and think what to do about it and then decide.

What would she say if he told her he needed a fence for his yard or a sail for his boat? She couldn't tell him the boat was all right, which was what she wanted to do because that way she might have talked him out of expressing his need for her help. The only thing to do was to make an objective judgment of it and then either agree or disagree.

And thus she went on rehearsing with me how to treat her son as an equal, as a man instead of a boy, as someone who had the right to express a need. Rehearsal was very important for her, and what seemed like artificial behavior at first soon felt very natural. It was much more important to the mother to rebuild her relationship with her son than to prove to herself that she could be spontaneous while the two of them went on bitterly quarreling. As a matter of fact, she told him after several months that she had been coming to me and that she had rehearsed how to break the pattern that had created so much difficulty for both of them. He was amused and I think the fact that she tried so hard must have touched him and showed him that she too had needs and was afraid of losing their relationship.

There is a kind of rehearsal with special value for us, which we may call negative rehearsal. Dr. Louis Ormont taught me to use the technique with patients, and I sometimes use it in my personal life. Instead of brooding about whether someone you met will continue to like you after spending a day with you, ask yourself, How am I liable to offend that person? Be specific. If you discover a fear of embarrassing the other person by acting immaturely, ask yourself by what actions you may do this. List them. The clearer your picture of how you may do damage, the better guarded you will be against doing it. Many of us exist with the vague feeling that we are undesirable, but few of us ask ourselves precisely how do we make ourselves undesirable? By asking such questions, we would, in effect, be rehearsing what not to do, a process sometimes even more valuable than rehearsing what we want to do.

CHAPTER 19

How to Make a Complaint

MARGIE GETS A call from her husband ten minutes before he's expected home for dinner, and he says that he's bringing home a guest. She asks a neighbor to watch her child and rushes out to three stores to buy food. This is the fourth time in the month that he's brought home guests at the last minute, but though she's angry, she doesn't say anything. When the guest is gone, she asks her husband whether he loves her, and he says he does. They have sexual relations which she doesn't enjoy, and they go to sleep.

Next morning, in the hubbub of breakfasting and preparing to meet the world, she behaves as though all were forgotten. But it isn't. Margie feels distant from her husband and thinks of leaving him. To subdue her anger she tries to convince herself that he is kind and that she's been making a mountain out of a molehill. But then she becomes frightened that he's going to do the same thing again and trembles with rage.

Margie needn't have suffered the demoralization.

Had she asked her husband not to invite guests home without giving her warning, either he would have listened to her request or he would have refused to listen to it. If after listening, he were to acknowledge that he'd inconvenienced her, she would have felt greatly relieved. And even if he didn't acknowledge having caused her unnecessary difficulty, she would have restored her self-respect by making the request. Even if the other person would be unreceptive no matter how approached, we are well advised to make our objections, since by making them we clarify our own view of the difficulty. Failure to object to what we feel is disdainful treatment of us is a sanction of the person's right to mistreat us, a sanction likely to harm us even more than the mistreatment itself.

Her husband's inviting friends home for dinner without giving her warning was one of many acts which Margie felt were impositions but against which she didn't complain. The accumulation of such grievances causes a slow but predictable drain of people's drive and hopefulness, and of their ability to enjoy intimate relationships.

Like Margie, millions of people choose not to object to what they consider impositions, when objecting would greatly improve their lives. In all cases, at the least, it would give them the feeling that they deserved better treatment than they were receiving. Some of these people fear that making a legitimate complaint (and we should not shy away from the word "complaint" when complaining is what we are doing) may reveal a weakness of which the other person would take advantage.

A woman once told me that her husband's practice of talking about the motivations behind her minutest acts was very upsetting to her. She hadn't asked him to stop because she feared that objecting would be arming him with information which he would then use to taunt her. She was, however, unable to support her suspicions with past examples of his using such knowledge to abuse her. It turned out that her suspicions were based on experiences she had had prior to meeting her husband. She hadn't given herself the opportunity of seeing that her husband was unlike other men she had known, since she had repeatedly chosen to hide her vulnerabilities from him. From her vantage point, it seemed that objecting to any of his behavior would be revealing a vulnerability.

Many people elect never to complain because they mistakenly imagine that anyone who objects to behavior is a troublemaker or a shrew. More often than not, these people have grown up under the domination of a haranguing parent, and they would now rather suffer nearly any abuse than risk resembling the parent. Still others withhold their complaints out of fear that their love is unrequited and that they're worthwhile to the other person only upon the condition that they act compliantly. They go through life on tiptoes, suspecting that their mate is waiting for the opportune moment to tell them that the relationship is over; these people stand ready to make immense sacrifices to maintain a harmonious atmosphere, on the theory that discord would give their mate the opportunity he is waiting for.

Nearly all these people believe that they've already tried to voice objections plainly, and have come to the sad conclusion that they weren't listened to. In some cases, the person's expressions of dissatisfaction were vague; in others he has loaded his arguments with so many irrelevant and disagreeable comments that few would have listened to him patiently. Being unaware of these facts, there seems to him nothing he can do now except to stifle his dissatisfaction and suffer the consequences—or else retaliate. And thus he continues to suffer.

In an intimate relationship, when someone suffers as a result of another person's behavior, the sufferer nearly always knows better than the other person which actions are causing him difficulty. His pain has been a stimulus for him to identify these actions. Unless he speaks up, he can't be certain whether the other person knows that he's inducing pain at all, or whether the other person would care. And sometimes he can't even know whether the other person would be able to control his harmful activity if it were pointed out to him.

If he doesn't make his objection, he predisposes himself to think the worst, that the other person knew he was inflicting pain, wanted to inflict it, and would have disregarded his pleas for better treatment if he had made such pleas. By deciding against voicing objections, we convince ourselves that other people are acting with rancor. By our silence, we imprint in our own minds the belief that objecting to the other person's behavior would be pointless, and yet we would all be distressed if a loved one reached that conclusion about us, especially if we felt we had not been given a fair trial. Most of us don't want to go on inflicting pain, and yet we are all of us capable of harming people we love, unwittingly. It's an obligation of any friend to give us the chance to stop hurting him by telling us how we are doing so. Friendships go by the boards when complaints aren't made. Grievances mount, and it becomes harder to make objections without bitterness. If a close friend belittles you by the way he talks to you, it becomes your responsibility to tell him precisely how he is doing so, and to give him the opportunity to show good faith by being receptive to your complaint.

Unless we are sure that our loved ones will tell us when we're causing them pain, when they are silent we can't be sure that we're not, and thus by persistent silence they rob us of the sense that we're pleasing them. Many an alcoholic has found it easier to suffer indignities than to voice his complaints and try to reconstruct his relationships. Finally, when the pain about which he had never complained grew intolerable, and his marriage seemed more than he could bear, he chose to drink to blot out his awareness that he was in a fraudulent life situation. When you want to preserve a relationship, being able to object fairly to behavior which you consider damaging to you becomes a necessity.

Another reason for learning how to frame objections has to do with the fact, already discussed, that disdainful treatment accumulates disdain. Where we wish to preserve someone's good opinion of us, we must do our best to stop him from treating us disdainfully. The longer we wait while people mistreat us, the less leverage we have when we finally do make our objections.

Complaining is an art as well as a responsibility. It's easy to say "Speak up," much easier than it is to speak up; and it's easier to speak up than it is to make an objection in a way that is fair and forceful and accurate. Like any art, that of making objections takes practice, and following new principles may feel unnatural at first.

Working with married couples over the years, I've evolved a set of suggestions, and have been astounded at how rapidly they've helped communication in many relationships. If you and someone else are quarreling regularly, I strongly suggest that you try them out. Perhaps you won't want to adopt them permanently, but they are very likely to bring peace for a time, during which you may decide which of them are helpful. I shall also make suggestions about how to accept a complaint. If the person to whom you make your objections is willing to follow them, your job will be easier; and if the two of you are willing to adopt both sets on a provisional basis, I think you will soon learn much about the source of the trouble between you. You may consider it a worthy plan to follow all the ground rules to be presented, in all your relationships. Making them habitual may help avoid many kinds of confusion.

1. Complain to the person you think is harming you, and not to anyone else.

2. Try not to object to your mate's behavior in front of anyone else.

To most people, being criticized feels like being personally attacked. Criticism is so often used as a vehicle for personal assault that it is not surprising they associate the two. Your indifference to your mate's comfort displayed by your willingness to criticize him in front of others will be taken at least as seriously as the content of what you say. In fairness to him and for your own sake, unless waiting would be costly for some special reason, wait till you are alone with him. Your mate deserves the chance to make his own impressions on people, without the shadow of your evaluations of him. This means that you're also doing him harm by praising him in front of other people.

3. Don't compare the person's behavior with that of other people.

Tell a girl that your former wife, Jane, wouldn't have kept you waiting so long, and you're almost sure to start a fight. No one wants to be described as inferior to anyone else. Comparisons will nearly always predispose other people not to listen to what you say, even where the complaint you want to make is justified.

Anyhow, comparisons of this kind are always irrelevant. Our standard for our own performance must not be based on what other people do, but on what we believe we can do. Therefore, the attempt to whip someone into submission by comparing him with other people misses the point. And beware of implied comparisons, like those conveyed by expressing disappointment with someone. The disappointing person is being compared with his better self.

4. Make your complaint as soon as you can; that is, as soon as you're alone with the other person and can articulate it.

Speaking up, like any task, becomes more difficult when you postpone it. Waiting allows your anger to build, and increases the likelihood that you'll make irrelevant comments. If you criticize someone for what he did long ago, you will look like a brooder. The impression will be accurate, and the other person will feel less comfortable with you afterward.

5. Don't repeat a point once you've made it and the other person has carefully considered it. This means, Don't expect a signed confession after you've spoken.

The reward for patiently listening to criticism ought to be exoneration from having to hear the same crime discussed again. A person's action against you either warrants ending the relationship with him, or it doesn't. If it doesn't, be a sport! Don't keep reminding him of whatever you think he did wrong, once you have brought the act to his attention and told him your reactions. I've worked with couples who had spent years rehashing each other's violations of their relationship; and they repeated their arguments, almost word for word as before, in my office. Usually I suggest a statute of limitations according to which each person can make whatever objections he wants to, but make them only once. He must make them within twenty-four hours of the offense, the time to be counted from when the two people are alone. As days go by, they must reduce the time interval when objections are allowable, until it is as little as a half hour. Objections which have not been voiced during the allowable period become null and void after it. The plan has two immediate advantages. It forces people to verbalize objections by taking away their reward for being silent; it gives to people who are unsure whether they've offended the knowledge that after a given time interval they need not fear rebuke.

Nearly always, the people who've been arguing accept my recommendation immediately, not realizing how heavily they've depended on citing other people's abuses of them as a way of defending themselves. When trouble erupts between them, both of them feel bereft of requisite weapons. Either they break their pact, or wait for the other person to break it, and then they barrage him with their store of references to his past. Practice is needed to resist this temptation. However, when two people can manage to desist from referring to one another's past as an argumentative device, they frequently discover that they don't have enough information left to sustain arguments like those that kept them up late into the night.

6. Object only to actions that the other person can change.

Your comments will be constructive only if they pertain to behavior the other person can change. You may ask a person not to shout, but if you ask him not to be angry with you, you're probably asking too much. I always ask patients who wear sunglasses to take them off in my office, both for their sakes and for mine, since I can make better contact with people when I can see their eyes. But though nervousness is often the reason that these people come to my office with sunglasses, it would be pointless for me to ask them to relax.

7. Make your complaints vocally, not facially.

A yawn has ended many a party, and a hangdog look has made many a husband wonder what he did wrong. Certain employers are experts at looking downcast when even their most dedicated workers decide that it's time to go home. At the end of a ten-hour work day, when you walk past one of them on your way to the door, he may look at you sadly, as though you've broken an intimate pact with him.

Facial expressions sometimes succeed in getting people to do what they don't want to do, but we don't look forward to meeting the people who bully us by sighing or acting disappointed with us. The fact that the victims of facial expressions seldom identify the tactic being used against them is undoubtedly what commends the tactic to its users. After a while, though, the user loses awareness of how he is influencing other people, and his face becomes his misfortune.

Facial expressions of all kinds are outward complements of the spirit. Our expressions may be rich and various, but they cease to be when we use them as devices to convey messages we are reluctant to put into words.

8. Try to make only one complaint at a time.

If you make more, you'll demoralize the other person, and perhaps obscure your major point. Don't quibble about the carpeting in your office when you've stormed in to ask your boss for a well-deserved promotion. If the subject changes to the price of carpets you'll feel unsatisfied; and your boss may feel he's discharged his obligation by promising to have your carpet changed.

9. Don't preface your complaint.

"Listen. There's something I've wanted to tell you for a long time. It may hurt you badly, but please don't feel offended by what I'm going to say..."

"I want to tell you something, and it's for your

own good. Now listen carefully to what I'm going to say..."

What could be worse than a preface like either of these? Instead of inoculating your listener against the pain of what you are going to tell him, you are stabbing him to death with your hypodermic needle. By prefaces, you convince both him and yourself that your complaint is to be monstrous and that probably he won't be capable of receiving it with the same friendly spirit that you feel while making it. There are perhaps as many people killed by prefaces as by complaints.

10. Don't apologize for your complaint after making it.

Telling the person you're sorry you had to disagree with him is apologizing for what you said in good faith. Apologizing is asking the other person to brace you so that you won't fall down under the stress of disagreeing with him. Doing so imposes an unnecessary burden on him; it will detract from the merit of your accomplishment, in your own mind, and renew your conflict about whether you had the right to say what you did.

11. Avoid sarcasm.

Among the invariable motivations for sarcasm are contempt and fear. Your contempt will predispose the other person not to heed you, and because you are making a choice not to confront him directly, you are intensifying your fear of him. Being sarcastic is sniveling, no matter how clever your turn of phrase. Sarcastic people have no dignity. They are cowards.

12. Don't ask people *why* they're doing something to which you object. Ask them to stop, if that is the underlying idea you wish to express.

"Why are you interrupting me?" "Why are you putting your feet on my chair?" It's obvious in each case that the speaker wants the other person to stop an activity. Probably, he doesn't feel strong enough to make the request openly. He cloaks it as a scientific inquiry. The question is worse than an inaccurate articulation of what is wanted. It would be easier for the other person to stop what he was doing than to search for his motivation and report it accurately to you. Many people regard serious questions about their motivations as obnoxious invasions of their privacy.

13. Rehearse your presentation if you need to.

14. Don't talk about other people's motivations when objecting to an activity.

Tell them simply what they are doing; and, if it is relevant, why you feel they ought not do it. Here are examples of statements that are objectionable because they include irrelevant speculations about the motives of the offender:

"You never *want* me to finish what I'm saying."
"You *don't care* how long I wait for you."

"Quit *trying* to make me angry."

If you stop playing psychoanalyst with people, and tell them how they're offending without giving them diagnoses, they'll become much more receptive to what you say. Each of the statements mentioned runs an unnecessary risk. It gives the listener reason to disregard your essential complaint if he concludes that your speculation about his motive is wrong.

Statements like these are irritating invasions of the listener's privacy. Hardly a man is now alive who doesn't feel the difference between, "Please don't interrupt me," and "You never want me to finish what I'm saying."

Look out for the tendency to confuse consequence and intention. The fact that someone is stepping on your foot doesn't logically imply that his intention was to hurt you. It may have been. But it may not. As I mentioned, Edward's father was plunged in sorrow over his gambling. But to assume that Edward planned a life calculating that effect would be to credit him with more purpose and resourcefulness than he had brought to bear. The ascribing to people uncanny power which they are supposedly using to harm us is a dangerous practice. This was precisely the assumption made in previous centuries to justify the burning of people as demons and witches.

15. Avoid words like "always" and "never"; they contain implicit references to the past.

Exaggerations intended for emphasis when making

an objection rob you of accuracy, and of all the psychological advantages that go with it.

16. If you never compliment the other person, don't expect him to remain open to your criticisms.

There was supposedly a little girl who didn't talk till she was eight. Doctors, social workers, and psychiatrists were all consulted but couldn't figure out why. Then one day at breakfast she cried out, "This oatmeal is lumpy." When asked why she had never spoken before, she answered that up till then everything had been all right.

Don't be this little girl. Complaints ring loud and long when they're the only sounds that are made. If you want to make occasional objections, you have the obligation to compliment the person at other times. And I recommend the practice of thanking people for listening to your criticisms.

Some Suggestions for Listening to Criticism

Most of us associate being criticized with being punished or told we're unwanted, and often it bears this implication, especially when parents criticize their children. Only by forcing ourselves to listen to criticism can we teach ourselves that it is sometimes well intended, and that we won't fall to pieces no matter what other people say about us.

1. Be quiet while you're being criticized and make clear that you are listening

2. Look directly at the person talking to you.

Only in this way can you convey open reception to what he is saying. Whether you agree with it or not is an issue to be discussed later on.

3. Under no condition find fault with the person who has just criticized you.

If he's made a mistake in grammar, wait a half hour before telling him. It probably won't seem so important to you then.

4. Don't create the impression that the other person is destroying your spirit.

Unless you suffer near-collapse when criticized, you needn't give off the message that you feel as though you were being beaten over the head. The hardest people to deal with are those who are belligerent at first, and who then, when cornered, act as though they were at the edge of despair. Don't be a fragile bully.

5. Don't criticize the other person's reaction to your behavior; for instance, by calling him oversensitive. *His* reaction is not the point.

6. Don't jest.

Flippancy is properly perceived as contemptuous by a great many people, and is hurtful to everyone.

7. Don't caricature the complaint.

If a person says you were *thoughtless*, don't ascribe to him the statement that you were *vicious* and then defend yourself against a charge he didn't make. If he exaggerates, don't seize his exaggeration and take it literally. The deliberate exaggeration of a charge against you amounts to dismissal of the charge.

8. Don't change the subject.

9. Use your intelligence to help articulate the objection, not to obscure it.

After giving a speech at Columbia University, Bertrand Russell was answering questions from the audience. One student's question brought him to a full stop. For a whole minute he said nothing, his hand over his chin, in thought. Then he peered at the student and rephrased the question, making it sharper and more precise. He asked the student, "Would you say that this is still your question?" and the student answered delightedly, "Yes." Again Lord Russell thought, this time even longer, nodding his head and twice seeming about to speak. Then looking toward the student, who was in a row far behind me, he said, "That's a very good question, young man. I don't believe I can answer it." A demonstration by a genius of how to use one's intelligence to help someone find a possible flaw in one's own reasoning! The reward: the discovery of the flaw.

The student who posed the question, a young philosophy instructor, was a hero afterward. I remember him smiling as he walked out of the auditorium surrounded by colleagues. But could he have done what Lord Russell did? And to what extent is genius composed of abilities like the one Lord Russell demonstrated?

10. Don't imply that your critic has some ulterior, hostile motive for making his objection.

If you are asking why the other person has objected to your act, you are not dealing with his objection. The question about him should come later, if ever. Perhaps he doesn't know his motive. That fact ought not to deprive him of the right to object to something you do.

11. Convey to the other person that you understand his objection.

Paraphrasing it is one good way of doing this. You are saying in effect that you have received the message and duly noted it.

If you observe the rules I've given, I think you have the right to ask your critics to try to observe all those listed for complainants. Don't let people carp at you on the pretext that they're giving you constructive criticism. You can distinguish carping from criticism by determining whether the other person stays within the rules for making a reasonable objection. I think you have the right at any time to ask for a short suspension of criticism. Refusal to grant it, or inability to tolerate it, betrays the compulsive critic. The ideal path is narrow: you must remain open to criticism but not allow yourself to be tyrannized by it.

CHAPTER 20

Personal Values and Personality

You owe it to yourself to decide upon a code of personal ethics which you consider humane, to adopt it, to reconsider it from time to time, and to strive to uphold it. You won't always win friends by acting in accordance with your code; in fact, you'll antagonize people from time to time. I'm not advocating observance as a method of winning esteem, now or in an afterlife. I am saying simply that ethical behavior can often produce effects on your psyche which are difficult, or perhaps impossible to produce in any other way.

A patient of mine, a mathematician teaching in college, told me he had bought a stolen automobile from a friend. He felt no responsibility, he said, since the car had been stolen by someone that even his friend didn't know, so that he was the second purchaser. My patient was at the time writing his Ph.D. thesis on Blaise Pascal, the seventeenth-century mathematician, philosopher, and religious writer, whom my patient revered for his purity and originality.

I asked him, "Do you think Pascal would have bought the stolen car?" And he laughed.

He couldn't say at first why the comparison seemed ludicrous. Further discussion revealed that though he had never put the thought into words, he had always taken for granted that he was as inferior to Pascal in ethical willingness as in ability to do mathematics problems.

I asked him what he would do if a friend inquired of him where he had gotten the car and how much he had paid for it. He said at first that he would not feel uncomfortable, then said he might, and that he hadn't thought about it before. Feeling exposed perhaps, he launched a lecture at me to the effect that to live in this culture you must use your wits where you can. I asked him how much he thought he had made during the year using his wits with techniques like the purchase of the car. "About four hundred dollars" he said. That year he had earned eleven thousand dollars, and his wife earned eight.

For the saving of four hundred dollars, what amounted to roughly twenty-four hours of work during the year for him, he had been willing to sacrifice personal force, belief in his own honesty, conviction of the values needed to enforce justice among his children, who quarreled incessantly, and some of his capacity for indignation, which he would need when wronged. He had in addition risked embarrassment among his friends, and even taken the one in a thousand risk of being arrested by the police for possessing a stolen car. By acts like this one he was dulling the force behind a complex system of beliefs which he had held as a child. Chief among them was the belief that justice is worth fighting for, even though it doesn't always prevail. And this belief, regarding the *ought* of justice, is more important for mental health than nearly any other, being intimately connected with our belief in the inherent dignity of man. If justice ought to prevail, man has inherent dignity; and if not, he has none.

Some of the arguments for being ethical a child can verify. Yet parents, succumbing to the myth that happiness comes from winning good appraisals, sometimes find difficulty justifying their demands that their children act honestly. Preoccupied as we are with deriving self-esteem from other people's esteem of us, we have actually allowed ourselves to adopt a taboo against telling someone to be ethical for his own sake. And yet there is perhaps no more successful way of living than by carefully defining a value system, examining it from time to time, and upholding it. Among its numerous advantages, a code of ethics provides us with exemption from too great a dependence on other people's opinions of us.

Among the more predictable penalties of defective adherence to our ethical standards is a biasing in our selection of friends, and even casual acquaintances. Our code, which influences a multitude of choices we make in everyday life, operates as a sieve, through which we may admit honest and passionate people, or systematically filter such people *out* of our lives. A girl told me during a therapy hour that she had made a telephone appointment with a young man who was to call her between five o'clock and six, the hour she was with me. She smiled, and said she guessed he wasn't the sort who would call on time; he would probably call her late that night. Notice the negative sieve effect—one act in a selection process by which the girl attracted men with little expectation of her, and disappointed the others.

Our value system determines the people who become important to us, whose judgments matter; and thus if we want these people to possess particular qualities, we had better take pains to give those qualities an important place in our thinking, and in our actions. This means if we want those critical people to be kind, we must make kindness important to us.

We have all on occasion excused unethical behavior on the grounds that the person who acted was suffering from psychological disturbance of some sort. Yet there is a taboo against believing that breaches of ethics, like disloyalty to a friend, can damage us psychologically. Since acts like lying can affect the psyche, we must acknowledge this fact, even if people whom we consider naive are opposed to lying for other reasons. If the real argument against lying is that it renews or intensifies fear, can produce demoralization and muddy our own vision, we must not hesitate to oppose lying on the grounds that it is harmful to us.

The simple truth is that we have not guarded against the decline of optimism and the loss of interest in life unless we have adopted some carefully considered code of ethics and are working to uphold it.

The study of how our actions affect us brings us inevitably to the need for a code of ethics. We cannot live without some value system; and for the sake of our own stability we must adhere to the ethics dictated by whichever system we choose. Since our code of ethics contains our most important attitudes toward other people and toward ourselves, we ought to consider it carefully and reconsider it often. Real sophistication is the discovery that other people's admiration will not lift us as we had hoped, and that the strongest argument for any behavior is its effect on us and our view of our fellow man.

CHAPTER 21

Mental Health and Personal Goals

THOUGH WE DIFFER in aspirations, it is possible to set down a list of attainments that most of us would consider desirable. Undoubtedly, most of us would agree that pleasure is preferable to pain, that being productive is pleasurable, that being effective with people is better than being awkward with them, that enjoying one's job is better than loathing it. Few of us want to suffer from compulsions, and it's safe to assume that most of us would like to avoid the torments of paranoia. Most of us want to be able to express love, and to be able to enjoy being loved. More often than we think, our problem is not inability to get people to love us, but inability to open ourselves sufficiently to experience their feelings for us. It is also important to most of us to be able to express kindness, and in that way make ourselves feel deserving of the sympathy of mankind—feel part of a legion that would be wise not to leave us behind.

Being able to articulate a goal helps us keep it in mind and make the choices, on the spot, that move us toward the goal; and therefore I'd like to mention some ambitions of my own which I think may be widely shared but not frequently enough articulated. I put high on my personal list the ability to act without observing myself and running a mental commentary about what I am doing. Also, the ability to remain alone for extended periods of time without depending on tranquilizers or distractants. Many people find it difficult to be alone. In efforts to prolong their contacts with other people, they tolerate harsh treatment without a whimper and allow it to avalanche until relationships become unbearable for them; or else, in their dogged demands for other people's time, they brush aside evidence that they're overstaying their welcome, and then find themselves alone for more hours than the rest of us do.

Also high on the list, I think, ought to be the ability to allow other people freedom. In the strictest sense, each of us makes all his decisons unilaterally, but when we're not careful we may use subtle pressures which goad people into the choices we want them to make. The price for this may be serious. When we deliberately convey our personal needs to people to win their sympathy and acceptance, or to make sure they spend time with us, we inevitably feel that they're responding to the undercurrent of our plea, and their interest in us feels unsatisfactory. It becomes hard for us to feel wanted by them. If they also spend time with people who don't make subtle demands on them or prey on their consciences as we do, we are almost sure to suspect that our relationship with them is less substantial than their other relationships, that there is a mainstream of free and spontaneous pleasure between them and other people to which we are forever denied access.

Next is the goal of avoiding deceptions in presenting ourselves. We must make it possible for our intimates to love us instead of illusions about us which we have produced. To do this, we must avoid retouchings if we can; sustaining hoaxes separates us from other people. I wouldn't want my best friends thinking I spoke five languages fluently unless I did; and I would be more uncomfortable if I had given them that impression than if they had arrived at it themselves. I've seen people brag about promotions they got after hard work, and by exaggerating the amounts of their raises, make themselves feel fraudulent when there was every reason to rejoice. Distortions are burdensome to reproduce; they confuse us about the genuineness of our receptions, and they leave us vulnerable to anxiety. We ought to evaluate jobs and relationships partly by how much pretense they demand of us.

It is also important, I think, that we acknowledge our role as final judges of our own behavior. Once we give to other people the ultimate power to judge us, if they set their standards too high, we are sure to feel beaten; and if they set them too low, we must feel that our accomplishments are empty.

There's a concept connected with mental health

that has valuable meaning for us—stability. Being stable doesn't assure us of being mentally healthy but stability, if we define the word precisely, would seem almost a requisite for mental health, no matter which other set of criteria we hold important. We are stable if our character structure perseveres relatively unchanged—that is, if we continue to renew roughly the same set of attitudes. Whenever we undertake to change our personality, we must make ourselves unstable for a time. The disequilibrium we experience as anxiety; and, if we wish to change, only repetition can help us reduce that anxiety.

The concept of stability is, in a sense, more elemental than any other we can apply in the study of personality. For instance, it is much easier to define stability than mental health, since instability reflects itself as anxiety, whereas people's ambitions for themselves differ so widely that it is hard to get even loose agreement among experts on who the mentally healthy person is. Remember that there is no official rule book making explicit what is healthy for you. Experts can suggest practical principles, but in the end you are the one who must test them out; you must use your own experiences to decide whether the experts' recommendations hold for you.

CHAPTER 22

Summary and Some Conclusions

I'VE PRESENTED A theory in this book. Naturally, an ocean of examples would be needed to fully demonstrate any theory with so large a claim; and I could do no more than to present generalizations which you, the reader, may test for yourself. I believe that the theory of action analysis is meaningful and accurate, that it can help us understand the significance our early childhood experiences had for us, and that it accounts in great measure for the consistency of our personalities. From the recognition that your personality resists being changed, you must not conclude that you are helpless to change it. There is much that can be done, and you can do it—by actions chosen with their motivations in mind. The important question to ask yourself when you undertake to change a personality trait is, By what actions am I renewing the trait?

Your thoughts and attitudes are to varying degrees special to you. Some of them are almost universally shared, and others, which you consider indisputable, are not nearly so obvious to people with different vantage points. My attention in this book has been given to the changing of thoughts and attitudes in some sense special to you. It may be said of nearly all such thoughts and attitudes that though they may seem fixed within you, they would not have survived if you had not refueled them by behavior. Nearly any long-standing attitude, like resentment of authorities, disgust toward your own body, or rage at criticism, if it persists owes its continued existence to choices over which you had control but whose significance you perhaps did not appreciate. Even guilt over an act that you committed many years ago falls into this category. It could not be present now were it not that you have all along been renewing it.

The implication is clear. We must study the way different patterns of action influence our psychic structure. The principles explaining how we sustain attitudes also explain how we can change them. The questions to ask about your childhood are not simply, How did your parents behave? or How did they treat you? but, What context did they create? and How did you choose to deal with it? While they fought bitterly at the dinner table, did you make a habit of looking at a spot on the wall to absent yourself, or did you argue with them? Or did you cry to stop them from quarreling and pretend you were physically ill? Very likely, you elaborated on whichever solution you found most effective then, perhaps still absenting yourself when there seems danger of open conflict, and renewing your belief, by a multitude of devices, that you can do nothing else at such times.

It is safe to say that in your childhood, whichever methods of survival you chose seemed reasonable to you. Quite naturally, you didn't appreciate that your actions would, in addition to securing your ends at the moment, regenerate the view of yourself which you held when you adopted your strategy for survival. The important issue is that you are here now, and if you want to alter personal traits or conquer emotional incapacities, there is no better way of doing it than by enlightened choices of action. You will be best equipped to make such choices if you (1) preserve your ability to identify your feelings of the moment, (2) understand the principles by which your behavior affects this pattern of attitudes, and (3) identify the particular activity patterns of yours which, though they may not have seemed important at first, are holding an unwanted set of attitudes in place. It is easier, in the end, to alter yourself directly than to alter your impression of yourself by winning acceptance or praise from other people and drawing your sustenance from it.

Sometimes it proves necessary to change seemingly insignificant traits before you can change others that are troublesome to you. The process may be regarded as the peeling away of layers of attitudes—a feat which you can accomplish by your behavior. You may find certain activities difficult or impossible to stop until you have released yourself from the drive by changing other activities. But don't confuse the need for a roundabout route with the impossibility of succeeding. In the past, you have found actions which were meaningful in terms of attitudes already present and those actions have further complicated your underlying attitudes; the process by which your present character structure came into being involved many steps, and therefore you may not be able to retrace your path in a single step. But if you work painstakingly, you will be able to retrace it, no matter how old you are.

The trend toward regarding behavior as the source of personality change is relatively new in psychology. Though the most famous behaviorist John Watson wrote a half century ago, it has not been until roughly the last ten to fifteen years that behavioral therapists have begun to assemble their data, and to devise treatment methods using their theories. However, these behavioral approaches have lost efficiency because they fail to take into account the importance of motivation. There can be no substitute for the therapist's understanding his patient's personal world, and for his developing all the qualities in himself that will allow him to do so. Today, most behavioral therapists regard themselves as in opposition to psychoanalysts, who have been our greatest students of motivation, and perhaps for this reason they have tended to underestimate the significance of motivation.

There are people who make the assumption that our character structure hardens in childhood and that nothing we do can change it; and these people may demoralize us with arguments that follow from their premise, if we don't know how to deal with them. You can report to such people having accomplished sweeping personality changes, and, proceeding from their pessimistic hypotheses, they will describe all such changes as illusory or superficial. They will tell you that though you *seem* to have changed, you are really the same underneath, and that the new attitudes and behavior which you report are merely new manifestations of underlying impulses which have not changed. It is easier to change than to satisfy these people that you have changed. Content yourself wth accomplishing your own personal ends, since by tricks of logic and the introduction of unverifiable hypotheses, the pessimist can always tell you that you have not helped yourself.

I once knew a little boy in danger of not being promoted because he was completely uninterested in his work and demanded the constant attention of adults. After a summer with a camp counselor who befriended him and helped build his confidence, he settled down. Today he is a trial lawyer, pleading cases for many clients who are poor as well as others very rich, and he tells me that the appreciation of all his clients is an important part of his recompense. To the pessimist, the little boy has not changed: he is the same rampant creature, yearning to be seen and praised, and has merely found a method of accomplishing his ends, one that society approves of. To the young man himself, now forty-one, his life was once a failure, but now it is happy.

From this same point of view, we could say that a little boy who was vicious to farm animals but who saw the inhumanity of his ways and grew up to become a surgeon has really not changed at all. We might say that in both roles he is expressing aggression, that his cutting people in the course of operations is merely a new outlet for his underlying hostile motive. However, to deny that such people have changed would, in the end, be to invalidate any definition of personality change that we could agree on.

The adoption of new activities is not synonymous with personality change, but enlightened choices of action can produce personality change; and you yourself, if you trust yourself, will be able to determine whether the changes you accomplish are real or illusory. Your reactions to yourself are more reliable than anyone else's theory; and if you don't think so, that is a problem which you ought to deal with.

In everyday life we all have occasion to assume that people can change; and if we keep this assumption in front of us, we shall not overlook personality changes when they occur. The better attuned we are to observing personality changes in ourselves and other people, the better aware we shall become of the actions that produce them, and the more control we shall have over our adult personality.

Much has been written about our inability to alter basic attitudes, not nearly enough about the harm we may do to our psyches by choices whose effects we do not consider. We all have occasion to adopt practices as means to our ends. The danger is that these practices often regenerate attitudes which, if we examined them closely, we would find less desirable than the attitudes we replaced. The trouble is we don't examine them, or else, if everyone around us seems to be undergoing similar changes, we ascribe these changes to maturity.

Was wearing attractive clothing originally one of your ways to get close to people, to get them to welcome you, to give you love? If so, one danger is that you have overinvested in clothes, to the extent that other people, whose presence might once have been rewarding, now seem unappealing to you because they can't possibly afford to dress as well as you. Was being intelligent a way to get an audience? And did you study at night to learn new words so as to impress someone and finally feel you belonged? If so, look out lest you've made a fetish out of what was once a means to an end. Was making money once part of your plan to buy time so that you could enjoy your friends. If so, are you making more than you ever dreamed you'd make but with no time for them? To put it generally, ask yourself whether you have, by renouncing what you once wanted most, and by intensifying desires for lesser fulfillments, denied yourself the opportunity for the richest possible relationships.

Ask yourself the question, What were your childhood dreams? Do they all seem foolish to you now? Perhaps they were idealistic, or unreasonable in their detail; but that doesn't mean the desires that underlay them were absurd. Most of us have surrendered our childhood dreams too readily. Instead of translating them into adult terms or trying to satisfy them approximately, we have given them up altogether. Just as we have given up trying to make the world what we once thought it should be, we have stopped trying to make our own lives what we once thought they could be. To the little boy watching the alcoholic, disheveled and stumbling in the street, it seems a miracle that any human being could arrive at such a stage. The miracle is that each choice we take modifies our subsequent view of ourselves and the world, so that *any* little boy, eager for adventure, for passionate and honest relationships, could, by a sequence of choices over a span of years, turn himself into that alcoholic. But we must rejoice at this miracle despite the tragedies it sometimes produces; for it means that each of us has the ultimate power to shape the psyche he will have in the future. It is up to us to study the ways our choices affect us and to learn to use the power in our actions to turn ourselves into the people we want to be.